THE
QUEEN'S
SPEECHES

THE QUEEN'S SPEECHES

Poignant and
Inspirational Speeches
from Queen Elizabeth II's
70-Year Reign

Hardie Grant

BOOKS

FOR HRH
QUEEN ELIZABETH II
1926–2022

THANK YOU FOR YOUR
KINDNESS AND SERVICE

Published in 2023 by Hardie Grant Books,
an imprint of Hardie Grant Publishing

Hardie Grant Books (London)
5th & 6th Floors
52–54 Southwark Street
London SE1 1UN

Hardie Grant Books (Melbourne)
Building 1, 658 Church Street
Richmond, Victoria 3121
hardiegrantbooks.com

Speech material compiled by Lucy York

Every effort has been made to trace or contact all
copyright holders. The publishers will be pleased
to correct any omissions or mistakes
at the earliest opportunity once notified.

Page 11: Getty Images/Staff via Getty Images;
page 35: Ray Bellisario/Popperfoto/Contributor
via Getty Images; page 53: AFP/Contributor
via Getty Images; page 75: Tim Graham Photo
Library/ Contributor via Getty Images; page 93:
Consolidated News Pictures/Contributor via
Getty Images; page 119: Tim Graham/Contributor
via Getty Images; page 143: Christopher Furlong/
Staff via Getty Images; page 176: Bettmann/
Contributor via Getty Images; back cover: Evening
Standard/Stringer via Getty Images

British Library Cataloguing-in-Publication Data.
A catalogue record for this book is available from
the British Library.

The Queen's Speeches
ISBN: 9781784886714

10 9 8 7 6 5 4 3 2 1

Publishing Director: Kajal Mistry
Acting Publishing Director: Emma Hopkin
Senior Editor: Chelsea Edwards
Design: Nikki Ellis
Proofreader: Caroline West
Production Controller: Gary Hayes

Colour reproduction by p2d
Printed and bound in China by Leo Paper
Products Ltd.

MIX
Paper from
responsible sources
FSC   FSC™ C020056
www.fsc.org

CONTENTS

ƎNTRODUCTION

On her 21st birthday in 1947, the future Queen Elizabeth II declared: 'my whole life whether it be long or short shall be devoted to your service'. The selection of her speeches gathered together in this book represents just a small portion of the many public addresses she made during her lifetime and is testament to the devotion with which she fulfilled that pledge. She made her first speech aged 14 and she was still speaking publicly aged 96. She attended countless state banquets and the openings of factories, schools and hospitals. She visited 117 countries on 290 state visits, travelling at least 1,032,513 miles and earning the nickname the 'million mile queen'.

The speeches included here have been abridged, and they have been chosen to reflect the breadth of topics and historic occasions that the Queen spoke about, and at, during her lifetime. A large portion of the book is taken up by her Christmas messages; they are the only speeches that she wrote herself, and it is these messages that reflect most clearly her own values. Recurring themes include the Commonwealth, tolerance, forgiveness, reflection and hope.

The Queen's public addresses through the decades track the huge technological and telecommunications developments of the age, something she showed a keen awareness of herself. She was brought up listening to the wireless and her first speech was given on the radio during the Second World War. Her 21st birthday speech was broadcast around the world from South Africa. Her first televised speech was in 1957, in an address made to the people of Canada, and for the first time in 1967 the televised Christmas speech was shown in colour. In 2012 the Christmas message was recorded for the first time in 3D. In 2022, during the Covid pandemic, the Queen made a virtual hospital visit to mark the opening of the Queen Elizabeth Unit at the Royal London Hospital via video call.

At times of distress, the Queen's speeches were a source of great reassurance and comfort. In 2013, it emerged that in 1983 a speech had been drafted by Whitehall officials for the Queen to give in the event of a nuclear attack on Britain. Luckily, that was one speech she never had to give, but she was called upon to address the nation when British troops went into battle in the Gulf War in 1991, on the eve of Princess Diana's funeral in 1997, and in 2020, when Britain was facing its first lockdown of the Covid pandemic.

In a thank you message following her Platinum Jubilee, given just three months before she passed away, the Queen said 'my heart has been with you all'. The speeches in this book show that to have very much been the case throughout her reign.

A NEW QUEEN

QUEEN

1940-1959

Princess Elizabeth was officially named Queen in 1952, but her first public address was made in 1940 at the tender age of 14. In the early 1950s she made several iconic speeches pledging her lifelong service to the Commonwealth. Soon after her Coronation, she and Prince Philip commenced their Royal tour, during which she would circumnavigate the globe, visit ten Commonwealth countries and make over 150 speeches. The decade also saw the first of her televised Christmas broadcasts, which became an enduring feature of her reign, bringing her annual personal messages into the homes of the nation and Commonwealth.

13 October 1940

Aged just 14, Princess Elizabeth's first public speech was a radio address to the children of the Commonwealth, many of whom had temporarily left their homes for safety during the Second World War. Her younger sister, Princess Margaret, joined her in wishing the children goodnight at the end.

In wishing you all 'good evening' I feel that I am speaking to friends and companions who have shared with my sister and myself many a happy Children's Hour.

Thousands of you in this country have had to leave your homes and be separated from your fathers and mothers. My sister Margaret Rose and I feel so much for you as we know from experience what it means to be away from those we love most of all.

To you, living in new surroundings, we send a message of true sympathy and at the same time we would like to thank the kind people who have welcomed you to their homes in the country.

All of us children who are still at home think continually of our friends and relations who have gone overseas – who have travelled thousands of miles to find a wartime home and a kindly welcome in Canada, Australia, New Zealand, South Africa and the United States of America.

My sister and I feel we know quite a lot about these countries. Our father and mother have so often talked to us of their visits to different parts of the world. So it is not difficult for us to picture the sort of life you are all leading, and to think of all the new sights you must be seeing and the adventures you must be having.

But I am sure that you, too, are often thinking of the Old Country. I know you won't forget us; it is just because we are not forgetting you that I want, on behalf of all the children at home, to send you our love and best wishes – to you and to your kind hosts as well.

Before I finish, I can truthfully say to you all that we children at home are full of cheerfulness and courage. We are trying to do all we can to help our gallant sailors, soldiers and airmen, and we are trying, too, to bear our own share of the danger and sadness of war.

We know, every one of us, that in the end all will be well; for God will care for us and give us victory and peace. And when peace comes, remember it will be for us, the children of today, to make the world of tomorrow a better and happier place.

My sister is by my side and we are both going to say goodnight to you.

Come on, Margaret.

Goodnight, children.

Goodnight, and good luck to you all.

21 April 1947

In a speech made on her 21st birthday, Princess Elizabeth dedicated her life to the service of the Commonwealth. It was broadcast on the radio from Cape Town, one of the stops on the Royal family's tour of South Africa.

I am thinking especially today of all the young men and women who were born about the same time as myself and have grown up like me in the terrible and glorious years of the Second World War.

We must not be daunted by the anxieties and hardships that the war has left behind for every nation of our Commonwealth.

I am sure that you will see our difficulties, in the light that I see them, as the great opportunity for you and me.

If we all go forward together with an unwavering faith, a high courage and a quiet heart, we shall be able to make of this ancient Commonwealth, which we all love so dearly, an even grander thing – more free, more prosperous, more happy and a more powerful influence for good in the world – than it has been in the greatest days of our forefathers.

To accomplish that we must give nothing less than the whole of ourselves. There is a motto which has been borne by many of my ancestors – a noble motto, 'I serve'. Those words were an inspiration to many bygone heirs to the throne when they made their knightly dedication as they came to manhood. I cannot do quite as they did.

But through the inventions of science I can do what was not possible for any of them. I can make my solemn act of dedication with a whole Empire listening. I should like to make that dedication now. It is very simple.

I declare before you all that my whole life whether it be long or short shall be devoted to your service and the service of our great imperial family to which we all belong.

But I shall not have strength to carry out this resolution alone unless you join in it with me, as I now invite you to do: I know that your support will be unfailingly given. God help me to make good my vow, and God bless all of you who are willing to share in it.

I DECLARE BEFORE
YOU ALL THAT
MY WHOLE LIFE
WHETHER IT BE
LONG OR SHORT
SHALL BE DEVOTED
TO YOUR SERVICE
AND THE SERVICE OF
OUR GREAT IMPERIAL
FAMILY TO WHICH WE
ALL BELONG.

QUEEN ELIZABETH II

25 December 1952

Queen Elizabeth's first Christmas message was broadcast live on the radio from her study at Sandringham, Norfolk. She paid tribute to her late father and asked the people for their prayers and support for her upcoming Coronation in June.

My father, and my grandfather before him, worked all their lives to unite our peoples ever more closely, and to maintain its ideals which were so near to their hearts. I shall strive to carry on their work.

Already you have given me strength to do so. For, since my accession ten months ago, your loyalty and affection have been an immense support and encouragement. I want to take this Christmas Day, my first opportunity, to thank you with all my heart.

Many grave problems and difficulties confront us all, but with a new faith in the old and splendid beliefs given us by our forefathers, and the strength to venture beyond the safeties of the past, I know we shall be worthy of our duty.

Above all, we must keep alive that courageous spirit of adventure that is the finest quality of youth; and by youth I do not just mean those who are young in years; I mean too all those who are young in heart, no matter how old they may be. That spirit still flourishes in this Old Country and in all the younger countries of our Commonwealth.

On this broad foundation let us set out to build a truer knowledge of ourselves and our fellowmen, to work for tolerance and understanding among the nations, and to use the tremendous forces of science and learning for the betterment of man's lot upon this earth.

At my Coronation next June, I shall dedicate myself anew to your service.

You will be keeping it as a holiday; but I want to ask you all, whatever your religion may be, to pray for me on that day – to pray that God may give me wisdom and strength to carry out the solemn promises I shall be making, and that I may faithfully serve Him and you, all the days of my life.

SINCE MY ACCESSION TEN MONTHS AGO, YOUR LOYALTY AND AFFECTION HAVE BEEN AN IMMENSE SUPPORT AND ENCOURAGEMENT. I WANT TO TAKE THIS CHRISTMAS DAY, MY FIRST OPPORTUNITY, TO THANK YOU WITH ALL MY HEART.

QUEEN ELIZABETH II

Throughout
this memorable
day I have been
uplifted and
sustained by the
knowledge that
your thoughts
and prayers were
with me.

QUEEN ELIZABETH II

2 June 1953

On the evening following her Coronation, The Queen made a broadcast thanking the public for their support. She reflected on the events of the day and promised to serve the nation.

Throughout this memorable day I have been uplifted and sustained by the knowledge that your thoughts and prayers were with me.

The ceremonies you have seen today are ancient, and some of their origins are veiled in the mists of the past. But their spirit and their meaning shine through the ages never, perhaps, more brightly than now. I have in sincerity pledged myself to your service, as so many of you are pledged to mine. Throughout all my life and with all my heart I shall strive to be worthy of your trust.

In this resolve I have my husband to support me. He shares all my ideals and all my affection for you. Then, although my experience is so short and my task so new, I have in my parents and grandparents an example which I can follow with certainty and with confidence.

There is also this. I have behind me not only the splendid traditions and the annals of more than a thousand years but the living strength and majesty of the Commonwealth and Empire; of societies old and new; of lands and races different in history and origins but all, by God's Will, united in spirit and in aim.

Therefore I am sure that this, my Coronation, is not the symbol of a power and a splendour that are gone but a declaration of our hopes for the future, and for the years I may, by God's Grace and Mercy, be given to reign and serve you as your Queen.

As this day draws to its close, I know that my abiding memory of it will be, not only the solemnity and beauty of the ceremony, but the inspiration of your loyalty and affection. I thank you all from a full heart. God bless you all.

25 December 1953

On Christmas Day 1953, The Queen and The Duke of Edinburgh were in Auckland, New Zealand, at the start of a six-month tour of the Commonwealth. The Christmas broadcast was recorded for the radio at Government House.

This will be a voyage right round the world – the first that a Queen of England has been privileged to make as Queen. But what is really important to me is that I set out on this journey in order to see as much as possible of the people and countries of the Commonwealth and Empire, to learn at first hand something of their triumphs and difficulties and something of their hopes and fears.

At the same time I want to show that the Crown is not merely an abstract symbol of our unity but a personal and living bond between you and me.

As I travel across the world today, I am ever more deeply impressed with the achievement and the opportunity which the modern Commonwealth presents.

Like New Zealand, from whose North Island I am speaking, every one of its nations can be justly proud of what it has built for itself on its own soil.

But their greatest achievement, I suggest, is the Commonwealth itself, and that owes much to all of them. Thus formed, the Commonwealth bears no resemblance to the empires of the past. It is an entirely new conception, built on the highest qualities of the spirit of man: friendship, loyalty and the desire for freedom and peace.

To that new conception of an equal partnership of nations and races I shall give myself heart and soul every day of my life.

I wished to speak of it from New Zealand this Christmas Day because we are celebrating the birth of the Prince of Peace, who preached the brotherhood of man.

May that brotherhood be furthered by all our thoughts and deeds from year to year. In pursuit of that supreme ideal the Commonwealth is moving steadily towards greater harmony between its many creeds, colours and races despite the imperfections by which, like every human institution, it is beset.

I WANT TO SHOW
THAT THE CROWN
IS NOT MERELY AN
ABSTRACT SYMBOL
OF OUR UNITY BUT A
PERSONAL AND LIVING
BOND BETWEEN YOU
AND ME.

QUEEN ELIZABETH II

25 December 1954

The Queen and Prince Philip spent 1954 travelling around the world, from Bermuda to Uganda. In her Christmas broadcast that year, made from her study at Sandringham, she celebrated the work of ordinary people.

In the turbulence of this anxious and active world many people are leading uneventful, lonely lives. To them dreariness, not disaster, is the enemy.

They seldom realise that on their steadfastness, on their ability to withstand the fatigue of dull repetitive work and on their courage in meeting constant small adversities, depend in great measure the happiness and prosperity of the community as a whole.

When we look at the landscape of our life on this earth there is in the minds of all of us a tendency to admire the peaks, and to ignore the foothills and the fertile plain from which they spring.

We praise – and rightly – the heroes whose resource and courage shine so brilliantly in moments of crisis. We forget sometimes that behind the wearers of the Victoria or George Cross there stand ranks of unknown, unnamed men and women, willing and able, if the call came, to render valiant service.

We are amazed by the spectacular discoveries in scientific knowledge, which should bring comfort and leisure to millions. We do not always reflect that these things also have rested to some extent on the faithful toil and devotion to duty of the great bulk of ordinary citizens. The upward course of a nation's history is due, in the long run, to the soundness of heart of its average men and women.

And so it is that this Christmas Day I want to send a special message of encouragement and good cheer to those of you whose lot is cast in dull and unenvied surroundings, to those whose names will never be household words, but to whose work and loyalty we owe so much.

May you be proud to remember – as I am myself – how much depends on you and that even when your life seems most monotonous, what you do is always of real value and importance to your fellow men.

25 December 1955

The Queen and Prince Philip spent most of 1955 in the UK, and they visited parts of the country they had not seen before. In her Christmas message broadcast live from her study at Sandringham that year, she focused on the opportunities arising from membership of the Commonwealth of Nations.

There are certain spiritual values which inspire all of us. We try to express them in our devotion to freedom, which means respect for the individual and equality before the law. Parliamentary government is also a part of this heritage.

We believe in the conception of a Government and Opposition and the right to criticise and defend. All these things are part of the natural life of our free Commonwealth.

Great opportunities lie before us. Indeed, a large part of the world looks to the Commonwealth for a lead. We have already gone far towards discovering for ourselves how different nations, from North and South, from East and West, can live together in friendly brotherhood, pooling the resources of each for the benefit of all.

Every one of us can also help in this great adventure, for just as the Commonwealth is made up of different nations, so those nations are made up of individuals. The greater the enterprise, the more important our personal contribution.

The Christmas message to each of us is indivisible; there can be no 'Peace on earth' without 'Goodwill toward men'. Scientists talk of a 'chain reaction' – of power releasing yet more power. This principle must be most true when it is applied to the greatest power of all: the power of love.

My beloved grandfather, King George V, in one of his broadcasts when I was a little girl, called upon all his peoples in these words: 'Let each of you be ready and proud to give to his country the service of his work, his mind and his heart.' That is surely the first step to set in motion the 'chain reaction' of the Powers of Light, to illuminate the new age ahead of us.

And the second step is this: to understand with sympathy the point of view of others, within our own countries and in the Commonwealth, as well as those outside it. In this way we can bring our unlimited spiritual resources to bear upon the world.

25 December 1956

On Christmas Day 1956 The Queen's broadcast from Sandringham was preceded by a short message from Prince Philip, who spoke on the radio from the Royal yacht Britannia, on which he was touring the Commonwealth. In her message The Queen spoke about the importance of unity.

If my husband cannot be at home on Christmas Day, I could not wish for a better reason than that he should be travelling in other parts of the Commonwealth.

One idea above all others has been the mainspring of this journey. It is the wish to foster, and advance, concord and understanding within the Commonwealth.

No purpose comes nearer to my own desires, for I believe that the way in which our Commonwealth is developing represents one of the most hopeful and imaginative experiments in international affairs that the world has ever seen.

If, as its Head, I can make any real personal contribution towards its progress, it must surely be to promote its unity.

We talk of ourselves as a 'family of nations', and perhaps our relations with one another are not so very different from those which exist between members of any family. We all know that these are not always easy, for there is no law within a family which binds its members to think, or act, or be alike.

And surely it is this very freedom of choice and decision which gives exceptional value to friendship in times of stress and disagreement. Such friendship is a gift for which we are truly and rightly grateful.

Nonetheless, deep and acute differences, involving both intellect and emotion, are bound to arise between members of a family and also between friend and friend, and there is neither virtue nor value in pretending that they do not.

In all such differences, however, there comes a moment when, for the sake of ultimate harmony, the healing power of tolerance, comradeship and love must be allowed to play its part.

I speak of a tolerance that is not indifference, but is rather a willingness to recognise the possibility of right in others; of a comradeship that is not just a sentimental memory of good days past, but the certainty that the tried and staunch friends of yesterday are still in truth the same people today; of a love that can rise above anger and is ready to forgive.

By bringing continuity and a sense of family to our richly diverse Commonwealth, the Queen has encouraged us to embrace positive change and fresh thinking, and to build together for the future.

PATRICIA SCOTLAND QC,
SECRETARY-GENERAL OF THE COMMONWEALTH OF NATIONS

21 October 1957

In October 1957, The Queen addressed the United Nations General Assembly in New York. She spoke about the goals of the UN and how the organisation relates to the Commonwealth.

This Assembly was born of the endeavours of countless men and women from different nations who, over the centuries, have pursued the aims of the preservation of peace between nations, equality of justice for all before the law and the right of the peoples of the world to live their lives in freedom and security.

The Charter of the United Nations was framed with a view to giving expression to these great purposes and so forming a fitting memorial to the men and women whose toil and sacrifices turned those ideas into articles of faith for the nations of today.

Time has, in fact, made the task of the United Nations more difficult than it seemed when the terms of the Charter were agreed at San Francisco 12 years ago. We are still far from the achievement of the ideals which I have mentioned but we must not be discouraged. The peoples of the world expect the United Nations to persevere in its efforts.

Ten Commonwealth countries are represented in this Assembly – countries which form a free association of fully independent states and which have widely different histories, cultures and traditions. Common ideals and hopes, not formal bonds, unite the members of the Commonwealth and promote that association between them which, in my belief, has contributed significantly to the cause of human freedom.

The countries of the Commonwealth regard their continuing association with one another and joint service to their high ideals as still an essential contribution to world peace and justice. They add and will continue to add to a tried element of strength, and of accumulated experience.

The United Nations is an organisation, dedicated to peace, where representatives from all over the world meet to examine the problems of the time. In it men and women from all these countries – large or small, powerful or weak – can exercise an influence that might otherwise be denied them. The United Nations also originates and inspires a wide range of social and economic activities for the benefit of the whole human race.

But, Mr President, the future of this organisation will be determined, not only by the degree to which its members observe strictly the provisions of the charter and co-operate in its practical activities, but also by the strength of its people's devotion to the pursuit of those great ideals to which I have referred.

When justice and respect for obligations are firmly established, the United Nations will the more confidently achieve the goal of a world at peace, law abiding and prosperous for which men and women have striven so long and which is the heart's desire of every nation here represented. I offer you my best wishes in your task and pray that you may be successful.

25 December 1957

The Queen's 1957 Christmas broadcast marked the 25th anniversary of the first Christmas broadcast on the radio and was the first to be televised. It was made live from the Long Library at Sandringham. The Queen reflected on the changes happening in technology and society and the importance of upholding some aspects of the old way of life.

It is inevitable that I should seem a rather remote figure to many of you. A successor to the Kings and Queens of history; someone whose face may be familiar in newspapers and films but who never really touches your personal lives. But now at least for a few minutes I welcome you to the peace of my own home.

That it is possible for some of you to see me today is just another example of the speed at which things are changing all around us. Because of these changes I am not surprised that many people feel lost and unable to decide what to hold on to and what to discard. How to take advantage of the new life without losing the best of the old.

But it is not the new inventions which are the difficulty. The trouble is caused by unthinking people who carelessly throw away ageless ideals as if they were old and outworn machinery.

They would have religion thrown aside, morality in personal and public life made meaningless, honesty counted as foolishness and self-interest set up in place of self-restraint.

At this critical moment in our history we will certainly lose the trust and respect of the world if we just abandon those fundamental principles which guided the men and women who built the greatness of this country and Commonwealth.

Today we need a special kind of courage, not the kind needed in battle but a kind which makes us stand up for everything that we know is right, everything that is true and honest. We need the kind of courage that can withstand the subtle corruption of the cynics so that we can show the world that we are not afraid of the future.

It has always been easy to hate and destroy. To build and to cherish is much more difficult. That is why we can take a pride in the new Commonwealth we are building.

In the old days the monarch led his soldiers on the battlefield and his leadership at all times was close and personal.

Today things are very different. I cannot lead you into battle, I do not give you laws or administer justice, but I can do something else: I can give you my heart and my devotion to these old islands and to all the peoples of our brotherhood of nations.

I believe in our qualities and in our strength, I believe that together we can set an example to the world which will encourage upright people everywhere.

25 December 1958

In her 1958 Christmas broadcast, made live from the Long Library at Sandringham, Norfolk, the Queen spoke about the importance of protecting children from public life while growing up, and the efforts of the Commonwealth to raise standards of living around the world.

Some of you have written to say that you would like to see our children on television this afternoon. We value your interest in them and I can assure you that we have thought about this a great deal before deciding against it.

We would like our son and daughter to grow up as normally as possible so that they will be able to serve you and the Commonwealth faithfully and well when they are old enough to do so. We believe that public life is not a fair burden to place on growing children. I'm sure that all of you who are parents will understand.

In recent years the Commonwealth countries have been making a great co-operative effort to raise standards of living. Even so, the pace of our everyday life has been such that there has hardly been time to enjoy the things which appeal to men's minds and which make life a full experience.

After all, our standard of living has a spiritual as well as a material aspect. The genius of scientists, inventors and engineers can make life more comfortable and prosperous.

But throughout history the spiritual and intellectual aspirations of mankind have been inspired by prophets and dreamers, philosophers, men of ideas and poets, artists in paint, sculpture and music, the whole company who challenge and encourage or who entertain and give pleasure.

To their number I would add the teachers in Church, school and university, whose enormous job it is to awaken the minds of the younger generations and instil into them the essence of our accumulated civilisation.

I am sure that many of you have thought about these things before, but it seems to me that Christmas is just the time to be grateful to those who add fullness to our lives.

Even so, we need something more. We all need the kind of security that one gets from a happy and united family.

1 July 1959

During a long tour of Canada, The Queen made a Dominion Day address from her Canadian residence at Rideau Hall. She praised the nation for having attained unity and noted that it was the first independent country in the Commonwealth.

Five hundred years ago there were no Europeans on this continent. Today, over 17 million Canadians enjoy what is probably one of the highest standards of living anywhere in the world. During the early history of what is now Canada there was controversy and fighting. Today you have achieved a unity and a sense of common purpose, which is a tribute to good sense and tolerance. This didn't come about of its own accord. It came about because there have been men in every generation who are not content simply to work for themselves, but who worked for the nation as a whole, who sacrificed their own interests for the common good. Dominion Day commemorates the birth of Canada as a nation and the first independent country within the British Empire. So it also marks the beginning of that free association of independent states, which is now known as the Commonwealth of Nations.

After all I have said, I'm sure you can understand why this tour has given me and my husband such pleasure, and why we are looking forward to the rest of it so much. I hope television will let you come with me to the different parts of Canada I am going to visit and see some of the spectacles and industrial developments along the route.

This is the holiday season for many of you, and a fine summer's day is just not the moment for serious matters, but I have spoken of these things because they are very close to my heart. If I have helped you to feel proud of being Canadian, if I have reminded you of the strength which comes from unity, and if I have helped to draw your attention to the bright vision of the years ahead, I shall feel well satisfied, because I believe that all of you living in this country can look to a glorious future.

STEADFAST
IN TIMES OF
CHANGE

1960–1969

In the 1960s, the world saw a great many changes. The Queen's annual Christmas messages were a reassuring bastion of continuity in these uncertain times, and they often touched upon current themes, whether discussing the evolving role of women in society or the launch of the world's first telecommunications satellite. The Monarch also offered words of solace at moments of great tragedy, including the assassinations of John F. Kennedy and Martin Luther King, Jr. The Commonwealth remained at the heart of everything, with a landmark Royal visit to India and acknowledgement of the many challenges that the member nations must work together to face.

25 December 1960

In this Christmas message, filmed at Buckingham Palace, the Queen gave words of solace amid troubled times at the end of a year in which an earthquake in Morocco had killed 12,000 people, 69 protesters had died in a massacre in Sharpeville, South Africa, and an explosion in a Welsh pit in Monmouthshire killed 45 miners.

By no stretch of the imagination can 1960 be described as a happy or successful year for mankind. Arguments and strained relations, as well as natural disasters, have all helped to produce an atmosphere of tension and uncertainty all over the world.

Although the causes are beyond the control of individuals, we can at least influence the future by our everyday behaviour. It is at times of change, disorder and uncertainty that we should cling most strongly to all those principles which we know to be right and good.

Civilisation as we know it, or would like it to be, depends upon a constant striving towards better things. In times of stress, such as we are living through, only a determined effort by men and women of goodwill everywhere can halt and reverse a growing tendency towards violence and disintegration.

Despite the difficulties there are encouraging signs. For instance in Africa, Nigeria has gone through the process of achieving full self-government in peace and goodwill.

This great nation of thirty million people has decided to remain a member of our Commonwealth and I know that her influence will be most valuable as the future unfolds in other parts of Africa.

Then, again, co-operation between Commonwealth countries grows every year and the understanding and mutual appreciation which is developing at the same time is one of the really bright spots in the world today.

Although the contribution which any one person can make is small, it is real and important.

Whether you live in one of the rapidly developing countries of the Commonwealth or whether you find yourself in one of the older countries, the work of mutual help and the increase of mutual understanding cannot fail to be personally satisfying and of real service to the future.

Although the contribution which any one person can make is small, it is real and important.

1 March 1961

On the eve of her departure from India, following a 23-day Royal tour of the independent Commonwealth nation, the Queen broadcast a farewell message over All India Radio. She thanked the Indian people for their welcome, praised the country for its progress and spoke of the new relationship between Britain and India.

I have always hoped that sooner or later I would have the good fortune to come to India. Now that this wonderful visit is drawing to an end, I have been thinking over all those things which will stay in my mind.

No one can fail to recognise that this country is dedicated to bringing about, within a democratic framework, a better, richer and happier life for every citizen. This is an immensely difficult and challenging task, and there would be no hope of success unless everybody was prepared to work and, if necessary, sacrifice themselves in this cause.

It is plain to see that, however much personal outlooks or backgrounds may differ, there is a deep underlying unity of purpose and effort.

I am also particularly heartened by the spirit of inquiry and of ambition which is to be found everywhere among your younger people. All over the world there is so much to be done for the less fortunate, and it is upon the young generation in every country that a tremendous responsibility will fall in days to come. We always welcome to Britain those from India who come to live and study among us, and who not only learn but also teach us something of their country. I hope to see even wider and deeper friendship developing between the youth of all our Commonwealth countries, so that the great varied talents which we have may be shared to our mutual advantage and to the advantage of the world.

This visit, and your great welcome to us, have set the seal on the new relationship between India and Britain and on the abiding friendship between the two peoples. It has also shown that the new Commonwealth, which came into being in 1947, is firmly based in the hearts and minds of the people as a means of co-operation for the peace and progress of mankind.

25 December 1961

In this Christmas message, made in Buckingham Palace, the Queen reflected on her travels that year to the Vatican City, Pakistan, Nepal, Iran and India, where she laid a wreath on Mahatma Gandhi's monument. She also spoke of the role of young people in building a better future.

Christmas may be a Christian festival, but its message goes out to all men and it is echoed by all men of understanding and goodwill everywhere.

During this last year I have been able to visit many countries: some were members of the Commonwealth and some were not. In all of them I was shown a genuine kindness and affection which touched me deeply and showed, I think, that the British people are looked upon as friends in many parts of the world.

In Asia and in Africa we were made aware of the great volume of goodwill and friendship that exists between all the varied peoples who profess different faiths and who make up our Commonwealth family. To them, their Christian brethren send a message of hope and encouragement this Christmas.

It goes also to the quiet people who fight prejudice by example; who stick to standards and ideals in face of persecution; who make real sacrifices in order to help and serve their neighbours.

'Oh hush the noise, ye men of strife, and hear the angels sing.' The words of this old carol mean even more today than when they were first written.

We can only dispel the clouds of anxiety by the patient and determined efforts of us all. It cannot be done by condemning the past or by contracting out of the present. Angry words and accusations certainly don't do any good, however justified they may be.

It is natural that the younger generation should lose patience with their elders, for their seeming failure to bring some order and security to the world.

But things will not get any better if young people merely express themselves by indifference or by revulsion against what they regard as an out-of-date order of things.

The world desperately needs their vigour, their determination and their service to their fellow men. The opportunities are there and the reward is the satisfaction of truly unselfish work.

25 December 1962

In her 1962 Christmas message, broadcast from Buckingham Palace, the Queen focused on the launch of Telstar, the first active communications satellite, which made it possible to broadcast television around the globe almost instantly.

Mankind continues to achieve wonders in technical and space research, but in the Western world perhaps the launching of Telstar has captured the imagination most vividly.

This tiny satellite has become the invisible focus of a million eyes. Telstar, and her sister satellites as they arise, can now show the world to the world just as it is in its daily life. What a wonderfully exciting prospect, and perhaps it will make us stop and think about what sort of picture we are presenting to each other.

Wise men since the beginning of time have studied the skies. Whatever our faith, we can all follow a star – indeed we must follow one if the immensity of the future opening before us is not to dazzle our eyes and dissipate our sense of direction.

How is it, people wonder, that we are forever seeking new worlds to conquer before we have properly put our own house in order.

Some people are uncertain which star to follow, or if any star is worth following at all. What is it all for, they ask, if you can bounce a telephone conversation or a television picture through the skies and across the world, yet still find lonely people living in the same street?

Following a star has many meanings; it can mean the religious man's approach to God or the hopes of parents for their children, or the ambition of young men and women, or the devotion of old countries like ours to well-tried ideals of toleration and justice, with no distinction of race or creed.

The wise men of old followed a star: modern man has built one. But unless the message of this new star is the same as theirs our wisdom will count for nought. Now we can all say the world is my neighbour and it is only in serving one another that we can reach for the stars.

25 December 1964

In 1964 anti-apartheid leader Nelson Mandela was jailed in South Africa, and Indian Prime Minister Jawaharlal Nehru died. In her Christmas message that year, the Queen spoke about the important role of the Commonwealth, in particular its role in overcoming the challenges of poverty and hunger facing some of its member nations.

I know that life is hard for many. The problems which face mankind often seem to defy solution. Some of our Commonwealth friends overseas are grappling with difficulties unknown in a complex industrial country such as Great Britain.

There are difficulties of over-population; there is hunger and drought and lack of power. There are yearly tens of thousands of young people flocking into schools, seeking education.

The thread which runs through our Commonwealth is love of freedom, and it is perhaps in this, more than in anything else, that our real wealth lies. Now the word 'freedom', like the word 'democracy', is a simple one implying a simple idea, and yet freedom, to be effective, must be disciplined.

Absolute freedom is a state unknown to the historian. The many ancient institutions and traditions which we have inherited, and which are familiar to us all, provide a framework and a dignified background to our way of life. If it is not to degenerate, freedom must be maintained by a thousand invisible forces, self-discipline, the Common Law, the right of citizens to assemble, and to speak and argue.

We do not wish to impose a particular form of government on any peoples in the world; we merely say, 'This is what we do; we know it's not perfect, but it is the best system that we have been able to create after many centuries of trial and error.'

All of us who have been blessed with young families know from long experience that when one's house is at its noisiest, there is often less cause for anxiety. The creaking of a ship in a heavy sea is music in the ears of the captain on the bridge. In fact, little is static and without movement there can be no progress.

Some speak today as though the age of adventure and initiative is past. On the contrary, never have the challenges been greater or more urgent. The fight against poverty, malnutrition and ignorance is harder than ever, and we must do all in our power to see that science is directed towards solving these problems.

14 May 1965

In 1965, a memorial to commemorate the life of President John F. Kennedy was erected at Runnymede, England, following his tragic assassination. At the inauguration, the Queen paid tribute to Kennedy as a champion of liberty.

Here at Runnymede 750 years ago Magna Carta was signed. Among our earliest statutes, it has rightly been regarded as the cornerstone of those liberties which later became enshrined in our system of democratic government under the rule of law.

This is a part of the heritage which the people of the United States of America share with us. Therefore it is altogether fitting that this should be the site of Britain's memorial to the late President John F. Kennedy, for, as leader of his great nation, he championed liberty in an age when its very foundations were being threatened on a universal scale.

We all recall how he welcomed this challenge and gloried in the fact that to his generation had been given the task of defending liberty in such a time of trial. His readiness to shoulder the burden and the passionate enthusiasm which he brought to his labours gave courage, inspiration and, above all, new hope not only to Americans but to all America's friends.

Nowhere was this more true than here in these Islands. With all their hearts, my people shared his triumphs, grieved at his reverses and wept at his death.

President Kennedy, together with his family, had many ties with our country. He and they lived among us in that doom-laden period which led up to the outbreak of war. The experience of those days led him to write, when still a young man, a most perceptive analysis of the predicament in which Britain found herself. Ever after he maintained a deep and steady interest in the affairs of this nation whose history and literature he knew and loved so well. His elder brother, flying from these shores on a hazardous mission, was killed in our common struggle against the evil forces of a cruel tyranny. A dearly loved sister lies buried in an English churchyard. Bonds like these cannot be broken and his abiding affection for Britain engendered an equal response from this side of the Atlantic.

The unprecedented intensity of that wave of grief, mixed with something akin to despair, which swept over our people at the news of President Kennedy's assassination, was a measure of the extent to which we recognised what he had already accomplished, and of the high hopes that rode with him in a future that was not to be.

He was a man valiant in war, but no one understood better than he that, if total war were to come again, all the finest achievements of the human race would be utterly consumed in the nuclear holocaust. He therefore sought tenaciously for a peace which, as he put it, would enable 'men and nations to grow and to hope and to build a better life for their children – not merely peace for Americans, but peace for all men and women; not merely peace in our time but peace for all time.'

Abroad, peace for a shrinking world; at home, a just and compassionate society. These were the themes of his Presidency. But it is his own example as a man that we remember today; his courage, both moral and physical; his dedication to public service: the distinction of heart and mind; the joyful enthusiasm, the wit and style which he brought to all he did; his love of liberty and of his fellow men. All these will continue to inspire us and the generations who succeed us and all those who share the noble traditions of freemen evoked by the name of Runnymede.

This acre of English soil is now bequeathed in perpetuity to the American people in memory of President John Fitzgerald Kennedy who in death my people still mourn and whom in life they loved and admired.

25 December 1965

The central theme of the Queen's Christmas broadcast in 1965 was family. She also spoke about volunteers and the important work they do, and the need for every individual to work to make the world a more peaceful place.

Christmas always remains as the great family festival. A festival which we owe to that family long ago which spent this time in extreme adversity and discomfort.

I think we should remember that in spite of all the scientific advances and great improvements in our material welfare, the family remains as the focal point of our existence. There is overwhelming evidence that those who cannot experience a full and happy family life for some reason or another are deprived of a great stabilising influence in their lives.

At Christmas we are also reminded that it is the time of peace on earth and goodwill towards men. Perhaps the most practical demonstration of goodwill towards men is to be found in the growing practice among young people to give some form of voluntary service to others.

In Britain and throughout the world they are coming forward to help old people or to serve in every kind of capacity where they may be needed at home and overseas.

A new army is on the march which holds out the brightest hopes for all mankind. It serves in international work camps, in areas hit by natural disasters or emergencies and in helping the poor, the backward or the hungry.

'Peace on Earth' – we may not have it at the moment, we may never have it completely, but we will certainly achieve nothing unless we go on trying to remove the causes of conflict between peoples and nations.

'Goodwill towards men' is not a hollow phrase. Goodwill exists, and when there is an opportunity to show it in practical form we know what wonderful things it can achieve.

To deny this Christmas message is to admit defeat and to give up hope. It is a rejection of everything that makes life worth living, and what is far worse it offers nothing in its place.

In fact, it is just because there are so many conflicts in the world today that we should reaffirm our hopes and beliefs in a more peaceful and a more friendly world in the future.

A NEW ARMY IS ON THE MARCH WHICH HOLDS OUT THE BRIGHTEST HOPES FOR ALL MANKIND.

QUEEN ELIZABETH II

THE DEVOTION OF
NUNS AND NURSES, THE
CARE OF MOTHERS
AND WIVES, THE
SERVICE OF TEACHERS,
AND THE CONVICTION
OF REFORMERS
ARE THE REAL AND
ENDURING PRESENTS
WHICH WOMEN HAVE
ALWAYS GIVEN.

QUEEN ELIZABETH II

25 December 1966

In her 1996 Christmas message, the Queen focused on women. The 1960s saw great changes for women, with their roles in society becoming increasingly important and prominent.

This year I should like to speak especially to women. In many countries custom has decreed that women should play a minor part in public affairs.

It is difficult to realise that it was less than fifty years ago that women in Britain were first given the vote, but Parliament was first asked to grant this one hundred years ago.

Yet, in spite of these disabilities, it has been women who have breathed gentleness and care into the harsh progress of mankind.

The struggles against inhuman prejudice, against squalor, ignorance and disease, have always owed a great deal to the determination and tenacity of women.

The devotion of nuns and nurses, the care of mothers and wives, the service of teachers, and the conviction of reformers are the real and enduring presents which women have always given.

In the modern world the opportunities for women to give something of value to the human family are greater than ever, because, through their own efforts, they are now beginning to play their full part in public life.

We know so much more about what can be achieved; we know that the tyranny of ignorance can be broken; we know the rules of health and how to protect children from disease.

We know all these things are important in our own homes, but it needs a very active concern by women everywhere if this knowledge is to be used where it is most needed. I am glad that in all countries of the Commonwealth women are more and more able to use it.

25 December 1967

The Queen's 1967 Christmas broadcast was the first to be shown in colour. It was the year that Canada celebrated the centenary of its Confederation, an anniversary marked by a five-week Royal tour of the country. In her speech The Queen also mentions Sir Francis Chichester, who that year became the first man to sail solo around the world in his boat, Gipsy Moth IV.

Every once in a while an event occurs which seems to mark a milestone in history.

For the Commonwealth, such an event was Canada's centenary this year. A hundred years ago the Confederation of the provinces of Canada laid the foundations for the country's subsequent development.

Once a land of pioneers largely dependent on agriculture and raw materials, Canada has become also one of the leading industrial nations of the world.

Prince Philip and I went to Ottawa for the centenary celebrations and it was a most moving occasion. Canada has every reason to feel proud of her achievements in the last hundred years.

Confederation as a formal act could have achieved little by itself. Only the determined will of a great variety of individuals and groups to co-operate for the greater national interest could have breathed life into the creation of the Fathers of Confederation.

The future of Canada as a great and prosperous country depends just as much on the will of the present generation to work together. It is for them to continue and expand the process of development which began with such high hopes one hundred years ago.

Great national events can stir the imagination, but so can individual actions. Few people can have attracted so much universal attention as Sir Francis Chichester during his epic journey in *Gipsy Moth IV*.

I am sure that the reason his great feat of seamanship so warmed our hearts was that we recognised in his enterprise and courage the very qualities which have played such a large part in British history and which we in these islands need just as much today and for the future.

25 December 1968

In 1968, civil rights leader Martin Luther King, Jr was assassinated in Memphis, USA. In that year's Christmas message the Queen chose the theme of brotherhood.

The words 'the brotherhood of man' have a splendid ring about them, but the idea may seem too remote to have any practical meaning in this hard and bustling age.

Indeed it means nothing at all unless the brotherhood, starting with individuals, can reconcile rival communities, conflicting religions, differing races and the divided and prejudiced nations of the world.

If we truly believe that the brotherhood of man has a value for the world's future, then we should seek to support those international organisations which foster understanding between people and between nations.

The British people together have achieved great things in the past and have overcome many dangers, but we cannot make further progress if we resurrect ancient squabbles.

The nations belonging to the Commonwealth have in their hands a well-tried framework for mutual help and co-operation. It would be short-sighted to waste this modest step towards brotherhood because we are too busy with the dissensions of the moment.

Every individual and every nation have problems, so there is all the more reason for us to do our utmost to show our concern for others.

Rich or poor, we all depend upon the work and skill of individual men and women, particularly those in industry and production who are the creators of wealth and prosperity. We depend on new knowledge, invention and innovation, practical improvements and developments, all of which offer us a better life.

Yet we should not be obsessed by material problems. We must also be sure that we remain spiritually alive. Everything we do now is helping to shape the world in which our children are going to live.

Today I have spoken of 'the brotherhood of man' and the hope it holds out for the world. This should not remain a vague thought nor an abstract idea. Each of us can put it into practice by treating one another with kindness and consideration at all times and in spite of every kind of provocation.

CELEBRATIONS AND STRUGGLES

1970–1979

Queen Elizabeth had much cause to celebrate in the 1970s, with her own 25-year wedding anniversary, her daughter Princess Anne's wedding, the Silver Jubilee and the birth of a new grandson. Many of the speeches in this section reflect on these happy and hopeful occasions. But it was also a decade that saw record inflation and unemployment worldwide, the intensifying of fighting in Northern Ireland and the rise of the Khmer Rouge in Cambodia. All was not well in the world, and reconciliation and goodwill were recurring themes in the Monarch's annual Christmas messages.

Never before has there been a group of independent nations linked in this way by their common history and continuing affection.

QUEEN ELIZABETH II

25 December 1970

The Queen reflected on her travels to Commonwealth countries along the route taken by Captain Cook 200 years previously. She spoke about the Commonwealth community and the many races it represents.

Every year we are reminded that Christmas is a family festival; a time for reunion and a meeting point for the generations.

This year I am thinking of rather a special family – a family of nations – as I recall fascinating journeys to opposite ends of the world.

During the course of these visits we met and talked with a great number of people in every sort of occupation, and living in every kind of community and climate. Yet in all this diversity they had one thing in common: they were all members of the Commonwealth family.

Early this year we went to Fiji, Tonga, New Zealand and Australia in *Britannia*. We were following the path taken in 1770 by that great English discoverer, Captain Cook.

A little later in the year we were in Canada, still in the Commonwealth, visiting the Northwest Territories and Manitoba for their centenaries.

Among people who are so essentially New Zealanders, Canadians or Australians, it struck me again that so many of them still have affectionate and personal links with the British Isles.

Wherever I went among people living in the busy industrial towns or on the stations and farms of the far outback, I met newcomers who reminded me that these links between our countries are renewed every year.

In Canada we met some of the older inhabitants – Indians – people whose ancestors were there for generations before the Europeans came. And further north still live the Eskimos, some of the most interesting people that we met during our travels this year. They too belong to the Commonwealth family, this remarkable collection of friendly people of so many races.

Never before has there been a group of independent nations linked in this way by their common history and continuing affection.

The strength of the Commonwealth lies in its history and the way people feel about it. All those years through which we have lived together have given us an exchange of people and ideas which ensures that there is a continuing concern for each other.

25 December 1971

In her 1971 Christmas message, the Queen focused on the theme of family. Footage included in the televised broadcast showed Prince Andrew and Prince Edward looking at a family photograph album.

Christmas is the time for families and for children, and it's also a time when we realise that another year is coming to an end.

As the familiar pattern of Christmas and the New Year repeats itself, we may sometimes forget how much the world about us has been changing.

It was 39 years ago that my grandfather, King George V, gave the first of his Christmas broadcasts. He spoke about a future which is now the past. Today it is our turn to think about the future.

Many of you who are listening are able, like me, to enjoy this Christmas with your families, and your children can enjoy the day as all children should. But tragically, there are many millions of others for whom this cannot be the same. Our thoughts and prayers should be for them.

Our children will be living in a world which our work and deeds have shaped for them. We cannot possibly tell what changes the next 40 years will bring. We do know that we are passing on to our children the power to change their whole environment.

But we also leave them with a set of values which they take from our lives and from our example. The decisions they take and the sort of world they pass on to their children could be just as much affected by those values as by all the technological wonders of the age.

The Christmas message is really one for all seasons and not just for one day of the year. If we can show this by our lives and by our example, then our contribution as parents will be just as important as any made by scientists and engineers.

Perhaps we can then look for the real peace on earth, and the powers which men have harnessed will be used for the benefit of our fellow men.

25 December 1972

In 1972, the Queen and Prince Philip celebrated their 25-year wedding anniversary. The Christmas broadcast that year included scenes from the celebration. The Queen spoke about the need for greater tolerance and understanding in light of the terrible violence unfolding in Northern Ireland.

My whole family has been deeply touched by the affection you have shown to us when we celebrated our Silver Wedding, and we are especially grateful to the many thousands who have written to us and sent us messages and presents.

One of the great Christian ideals is a happy and lasting marriage between man and wife, but no marriage can hope to succeed without a deliberate effort to be tolerant and understanding. This doesn't come easily to individuals and it certainly doesn't come naturally to communities or nations.

We know only too well that a selfish insistence upon our rights and our own point of view leads to disaster. We all ought to know by now that a civilised and peaceful existence is only possible when people make the effort to understand each other.

Looking at the world, one might be forgiven for believing that many people have never heard of this simple idea. Every day there are reports of violence, lawlessness and the disregard for human life.

Most of this is excused on purely selfish grounds. I know there are millions of kindly people throughout the world who are saddened with me for all those who suffer from these outrages.

In the United Kingdom we have our own particular sorrows in Northern Ireland and I want to send a special message of sympathy to all those men, women and children who have suffered and endured so much.

But there is a light in this tragic situation. The people are steadfastly carrying on their ordinary business in their factories and places of work.

Voluntary workers, both in and out of uniform, have struggled to keep humanity and common sense alive. The social services have done their job magnificently. The forces of law and order continue their thankless task with the utmost fortitude in the face of appalling provocation.

We must admire them greatly for their patience and restraint.

I ask you all to join me in praying that the hearts and minds of everyone in that troubled Province may be touched with the spirit of Christmas and the message of brotherhood, peace and goodwill. May tolerance and understanding release the people from terror and put gladness in the place of fear.

In the United Kingdom we have our own particular sorrows in Northern Ireland and I want to send a special message of sympathy to all those men, women and children who have suffered and endured so much.

QUEEN ELIZABETH II

25 December 1973

In 1973, the wedding of Princess Anne and Captain Mark Phillips was cause for much celebration. The Christmas broadcast featured film shot at Buckingham Palace on their wedding day. The Queen reflected on the happy occasion.

It is now 21 years since I first broadcast a Christmas message to the Commonwealth. Then our two elder children were only four and two.

Now, our daughter joins us for Christmas with her husband and we are celebrating the festival this year with the memories of their wedding very much in our minds.

We are constantly being told that we live in a changing world and that we need to adapt to changing conditions. But this is only part of the truth and I am sure that all parents seeing their children getting married are reminded of the continuity of human life.

That is why, I think, that at weddings all friends and relations, and even complete strangers, can stop worrying for a moment and share in the happiness of the couple who are getting married.

I am glad that my daughter's wedding gave such pleasure to so many people just at a time when the world was facing very serious problems.

People all over the world watched the wedding on television, but there were still many in London on the day, and their warmth and enthusiasm ensured it was an occasion my family will never forget.

Those of you who are surrounded by friends – or, of course, who are members of a happy family – know this makes life much easier.

Everything – the good and the bad – can be shared, but it is too easy for us to forget those who are not so fortunate.

However, there are many people of all ages who go out to help the old and the lonely, the sick and the handicapped. I am sure that, in so doing, they find the real happiness that comes from serving and thinking of others.

25 December 1974

The year 1974 saw continuing violence in Northern Ireland and the Middle East, famine in Bangladesh and floods in Brisbane, Australia. The Queen's Christmas message that year stressed the importance of working together.

We have never been short of problems, but in the last year everything seems to have happened at once. There have been floods and drought and famine; there have been outbreaks of senseless violence. And on top of it all the cost of living continues to rise – everywhere.

Here in Britain, from where so many people of the Commonwealth came, we hear a great deal about our troubles, about discord and dissension and about the uncertainty of our future.

Perhaps we make too much of what is wrong and too little of what is right. The trouble with gloom is that it feeds upon itself and depression causes more depression.

There are indeed real dangers and there are real fears and we will never overcome them if we turn against each other with angry accusations.

We may hold different points of view but it is in times of stress and difficulty that we most need to remember that we have much more in common than there is dividing us.

We have the lessons of history to show that the British people have survived many a desperate situation when they acted together.

People in a crowd may seem oblivious of each other. Yet if you look at your neighbours you will see other people with worries and difficulties probably greater than your own. It is time to recognise that in the end we all depend upon each other and that we are therefore responsible for each other.

25 December 1975

For the first time, the Queen's Christmas message was broadcast outdoors, from the gardens of Buckingham Palace. The year had seen record inflation and unemployment in the UK and worldwide. The Queen spoke of the difference an individual's actions can make and how this can shape society.

So much of the time we feel that our lives are dominated by great impersonal forces beyond our control; the scale of things and organisations seems to get bigger and more inhuman.

We are horrified by brutal and senseless violence, and above all the whole fabric of our lives is threatened by inflation, the frightening sickness of the world today.

Then Christmas comes, and once again we are reminded that people matter, and it is our relationship with one another that is most important.

We are all different, but each of us has his own best to offer. The responsibility for the way we live life with all its challenges, sadness and joy is ours alone. If we do this well, it will also be good for our neighbours.

If you throw a stone into a pool, the ripples go on spreading outwards. A big stone can cause waves, but even the smallest pebble changes the whole pattern of the water. Our daily actions are like those ripples, each one makes a difference, even the smallest.

It does matter therefore what each individual does each day. Kindness, sympathy, resolution and courteous behaviour are infectious. Acts of courage and self-sacrifice, like those of the people who refuse to be terrorised by kidnappers or hijackers, or who defuse bombs, are an inspiration to others.

And the combined effect can be enormous. If enough grains of sand are dropped into one side of a pair of scales they will, in the end, tip it against a lump of lead.

We may feel powerless alone but the joint efforts of individuals can defeat the evils of our time. Together they can create a stable, free and considerate society.

Like those grains of sand, they can tip the balance. So take heart from the Christmas message and be happy.

THEN CHRISTMAS
COMES, AND ONCE
AGAIN WE ARE
REMINDED THAT
PEOPLE MATTER,
AND IT IS OUR
RELATIONSHIP WITH
ONE ANOTHER THAT
IS MOST IMPORTANT.

QUEEN ELIZABETH II

25 December 1976

In 1976 the United States' bicentenary was marked by a state visit from the Queen and Prince Philip. In her Christmas message that year, the Queen reflected on their visit and spoke on the theme of reconciliation.

Christmas is a time for reconciliation. A time not only for families and friends to come together but also for differences to be forgotten.

In 1976 I was reminded of the good that can flow from a friendship that is mended. Two hundred years ago the representatives of the 13 British Colonies in North America signed the Declaration of Independence in Philadelphia.

This year we went to America to join in their Bicentennial celebrations. Who would have thought 200 years ago that a descendent of King George III could have taken part in these celebrations? Yet that same King was among the first to recognise that old scores must be settled and differences reconciled, and the first United States Ambassador to Britain declared that he wanted 'the old good nature and the old good humour restored'.

And restored they were. The United States was born in bitter conflict with Britain but we didn't remain enemies for long. From our reconciliation came incalculable benefits to mankind and a partnership which, together with many countries of the Commonwealth, was proved in two world wars and ensured that the light of liberty was not extinguished.

King George III never saw the Colonies he lost. My father, King George VI, was the first British Sovereign to see the famous skyline of Manhattan and to visit the rich and vibrant country that lies beyond it.

Wherever we went the welcome was the same, all the way to Boston, where the first shots in the war between Britain and America were fired.

Reconciliation, like the one that followed the American War of Independence, is the product of reason, tolerance and love, and I think that Christmas is a good time to reflect on it.

It is easy enough to see where reconciliation is needed and where it would heal and purify, obviously in national and international affairs, but also in homes and families.

It is not something that is easy to achieve. But things that are worthwhile seldom are, so it is encouraging to know that there are many people trying to achieve it.

Remember that good spreads outwards and every little does help.

PERHAPS THIS JUBILEE
IS A TIME TO REMIND
OURSELVES OF THE
BENEFITS WHICH UNION
HAS CONFERRED,
AT HOME AND IN
OUR INTERNATIONAL
DEALINGS, ON THE
INHABITANTS OF ALL
PARTS OF THIS UNITED
KINGDOM.

QUEEN ELIZABETH II

4 May 1977

The start of the Queen's Silver Jubilee celebrations were marked on 4 May 1977 with an address by the Queen to Parliament in which she reflected on her reign.

It is appropriate that I should come to Westminster at the start of the Jubilee celebrations in the United Kingdom. Here, in a meeting of Sovereign and Parliament, the essence of constitutional monarchy is reflected.

It is a form of government in which those who represent the main elements of the community can come together to reconcile conflicting interests and to strive for the hopes and aims we all share. It has adapted itself to the changes in our own society and in international relationships, yet it has remained true to its essential role. It has provided the fabric of good order in society and has been the guardian of the liberties of individual citizens.

These 25 years have seen much change for Britain. By virtue of tolerance and understanding, the Empire has evolved into a Commonwealth of 36 independent nations spanning the five continents. No longer an imperial power, we have been coming to terms with what this means for ourselves and for our relations with the rest of the world.

We have forged new links with other countries and in joining the European Economic Communities we have taken what is perhaps one of the most significant decisions during my reign.

At home there are greater opportunities for all sorts and conditions of men and women. Developments in science, technology and in medicine have improved the quality and comfort of life and, of course, there has also been television!

We in Government and Parliament have to accept the challenges which this progress imposes on us. And they are considerable.

Perhaps this Jubilee is a time to remind ourselves of the benefits which union has conferred, at home and in our international dealings, on the inhabitants of all parts of this United Kingdom.

A Jubilee is also a time to look forward! We should certainly do this with determination and I believe we can also do so with hope. We have so many advantages, the basic stability of our institutions, our traditions of public service and concern for others, our family life and, above all, the freedom which you and your predecessors in Parliament have, through the ages, so fearlessly upheld.

25 December 1977

In her Christmas broadcast of 1977 the Queen gave thanks to all those who attended her Silver Jubilee celebrations and expressed hope for reconciliation in Northern Ireland. In August she had visited the country for the first time in 11 years.

I shall never forget the scene outside Buckingham Palace on Jubilee Day. The cheerful crowd was symbolic of the hundreds of thousands of people who greeted us wherever we went in this Jubilee Year – in 12 Commonwealth countries and 36 counties in the United Kingdom.

But I believe it also revealed to the world that we can be a united people. It showed that all the artificial barriers which divide man from man and family from family can be broken down.

Last Christmas I said that my wish for 1977 was that it should be a year of reconciliation. You have shown by the way in which you have celebrated the Jubilee that this was not an impossible dream. Thank you all for your response.

Nowhere is reconciliation more desperately needed than in Northern Ireland. That is why I was particularly pleased to go there. No one dared to promise an early end to the troubles but there is no doubt that people of goodwill in Northern Ireland were greatly heartened by the chance they had to share the celebrations with the rest of the nation and Commonwealth.

Many people in all parts of the world have demonstrated this goodwill in a practical way by giving to the Silver Jubilee Appeal. The results of their kindness will be appreciated by young people – and by those they are able to help – for many years to come.

The great resurgence of community spirit which has marked the celebrations has shown the value of the Christian ideal of loving our neighbours. If we can keep this spirit alive, life will become better for all of us.

HER MAJESTY
HAS BEEN A PILLAR
OF STRENGTH,
INSPIRATION AND
UNITY, NOT ONLY FOR
THE PEOPLE OF THE
UNITED KINGDOM,
BUT FOR THE
COMMONWEALTH AND
THE WORLD AS
A WHOLE.

YOWERI KAGUTA MUSEVENI,
PRESIDENT OF THE REPUBLIC OF UGANDA

25 December 1978

The 1978 Christmas broadcast featured footage of the Queen with her new grandson, Peter Phillips, and Princess Anne, as well as recordings of earlier broadcasts made by King George V. In her message she focused on the theme of the future.

Now it is our turn to work for a future which our grandchildren will step into one day. We cannot be certain what lies ahead for them but we should know enough to put them on the right path.

We can do this if we have the good sense to learn from the experience of those who have gone before us and to hold on to all the good that has been handed down to us in trust.

Look around at your families as you are gathered together for Christmas. Look at the younger ones – they are the future and just as we were helped to understand and to appreciate the values of a civilised community, it is now our responsibility to help them to do the same.

We must not let the difficulties of the present or the uncertainties of the future cause us to lose faith. You remember the saying 'the optimist proclaims that we live in the best of all possible worlds, and the pessimist fears that this is true'.

It is far from easy to be cheerful and constructive when things around us suggest the opposite; but to give up the effort would mean, as it were, to switch off hope for a better tomorrow.

Even if the problems seem overwhelming, there is always room for optimism. Every problem presents us with the opportunity both to find an answer for ourselves and to help others.

The context of the lives of the next generation is being set, here and now, not so much by the legacy of science or wealth or political structure that we shall leave behind us, but by the example of our attitudes and behaviour to one another and by trying to show unselfish, loving and creative concern for those less fortunate than ourselves.

Christians have the compelling example of the life and teaching of Christ and, for myself, I would like nothing more than that my grandchildren should hold dear his ideals which have helped and inspired so many previous generations.

25 December 1979

In 1979, hundreds of thousands of refugees fled Cambodia in the wake of the rule of the Khmer Rouge. It was also named the Year of the Child. Children and young people were at the heart of the Queen's Christmas message.

It is an unhappy coincidence that political and economic forces have made this an exceptionally difficult and tragic year for many families and children in several parts of the world – but particularly in Southeast Asia.

The situation has created a desperately serious challenge and I am glad to know that so many people of the Commonwealth have responded with wonderful generosity and kindness. It seems that the greater the needs of children, the more people everywhere rise to the occasion.

My daughter, as President of the Save the Children Fund, saw some of these volunteers looking after refugee children in the Far East. Nowhere is the voluntary effort more active than in charities and organisations devoted to helping children to survive the hazards to which they have been subjected.

The Year of the Child has emphasised the value of this work, but we must not forget that every generation has to face the problems of childhood and the stresses of growing up, and, in due course, the responsibilities of parents and adults. If they are handicapped in themselves, or by their family or community, their problems are all the more difficult.

Children are born with a mixed package of emotions, talents and handicaps, but without knowledge or experience. As they grow up they have to learn to live with their parents and families; and they have to adjust to school, including the discovery of leisure activities and learning to handle their relationships with their contemporaries and with strangers.

Schools, charities and voluntary organisations and institutions can do a great deal to help, and I have admired their work in many parts of the world; but in the end each one of us has a primary and personal responsibility for our own children, for children entrusted to our care and for all the children in our own communities.

Focus on the Positive

1980–1989

The 1980s saw the United Kingdom go to war in the Falkland Islands. There were also multiple devastating natural disasters around the world and terrorist bombings in Northern Ireland. While showing sensitivity towards these difficult events, the Queen's Christmas messages sought to highlight the importance of celebrating good news and promoting tolerance and forgiveness. And there were occasions to celebrate, with the Queen Mother's 80th birthday, the christening of Prince Harry and the bicentenary of Australia. The Monarch remained ever conscious of technological developments and the opportunities these presented for the Commonwealth. She was also mindful of important issues such as taking steps to mitigate environmental damage.

25 December 1980

The Queen's Christmas message for 1980 mentioned the celebrations for the Queen Mother's 80th birthday that year and dealt with the theme of service in its many forms.

The loyalty and affection, which so many people showed to my mother, reflected a feeling, expressed in many different ways, that she is a person who has given selfless service to the people of this country and of the Commonwealth.

As I go about the country and abroad I meet many people who, all in their own ways, are making a real contribution to their community. I come across examples of unselfish service in all walks of life and in many unexpected places.

Some people choose their occupation so that they can spend their lives in the service of their fellow citizens.

We see doctors, nurses and hospital staff caring for the sick; those in the churches and religious communities; in central and local government; in the armed services; in the police and in the courts and prisons; in industry and commerce.

It is the same urge to make a contribution which drives those seeking the highest standards in education or art, in music or architecture.

Others find ways to give service in their spare time, through voluntary organisations or simply on their own individual initiative contributing in a thousand ways to all that is best in our society.

It may be providing company for the old and housebound; help for the disabled; care for the deprived and those in trouble; concern for neighbours; or encouragement for the young.

To all of you on this Christmas Day, whatever your conditions of work and life, easy or difficult; whether you feel that you are achieving something or whether you feel frustrated; I want to say a word of thanks.

And I include all those who don't realise that they deserve thanks and are content that what they do is unseen and unrewarded. The very act of living a decent and upright life is in itself a positive factor in maintaining civilised standards.

I MEET MANY PEOPLE
WHO, ALL IN THEIR
OWN WAYS, ARE MAKING
A REAL CONTRIBUTION
TO THEIR COMMUNITY.
I COME ACROSS
EXAMPLES OF UNSELFISH
SERVICE IN ALL WALKS
OF LIFE AND IN MANY
UNEXPECTED PLACES.

QUEEN ELIZABETH II

MEMBERS OF THE COMMONWEALTH ... HAVE ACQUIRED AN AFFINITY THROUGH SHARING A COMMON PHILOSOPHY OF INDIVIDUAL FREEDOM, DEMOCRATIC GOVERNMENT AND THE RULE OF LAW.

QUEEN ELIZABETH II

25 December 1982

In 1982 British troops went to war to defend the Falkland Islands in the South Atlantic. The Monarch's theme for that year's Christmas message was the sea. It was the 50th anniversary of the first Christmas message, and the broadcast was filmed in the library of Windsor Castle for the first time.

William became the Conqueror after invading England by sea. It was the voyages of discovery by the great seamen of Queen Elizabeth's day which laid the foundations of modern trade; and to this day 90 per cent of it still goes by sea. Discovery and trade in their turn laid the foundations of the present-day Commonwealth ...

Such names as Drake, Anson, Frobisher, Cook, Vancouver and Phillip are familiar to people in widely different parts of the Commonwealth – while in Britain we owe our independence to the seamen who fought the Armada nearly 400 years ago and to Nelson and his band of brothers who destroyed Napoleon's dreams of invasion.

Nor could the great battles for peace and freedom in the first half of the twentieth century have been won without control of the seas.

Earlier this year in the South Atlantic the Royal Navy and the Merchant Navy enabled our sailors, soldiers and airmen to go to the rescue of the Falkland Islanders 8,000 miles across the ocean; and to reveal the professional skills and courage that could be called on in defence of basic freedoms.

Throughout history, seamen all over the world have shared a common experience and there is a special sense of brotherhood between merchant and naval seamen, fishermen, lifeboatmen and, more recently, yachtsmen.

In much the same way, the members of the Commonwealth, which evolved from Britain's seafaring history, have acquired an affinity through sharing a common philosophy of individual freedom, democratic government and the rule of law.

It may not sound very substantial but when measured against the number and variety of inter-Commonwealth organisations and the multitude of commercial, medical, legal and sporting connections, it becomes clear that this common philosophy has had a very powerful influence for unity.

Nothing could have demonstrated this unity more vividly than the immensely reassuring support given to Britain by the Commonwealth during the Falkland Islands crisis.

25 December 1983

In her 1983 Christmas message, the Queen spoke about recent travel and communication developments, and how these developments presented new possibilities for co-operation within the Commonwealth.

In the year I was born, radio communication was barely out of its infancy; there was no television; civil aviation had hardly started and space satellites were still in the realm of science fiction. When my Grandfather visited India in 1911, it took three weeks by sea to get there. Last month I flew back from Delhi to London in a matter of hours.

Travel and communication have entered a completely new dimension. In Los Angeles I went to see the space shuttle which is playing such an important part in providing more and better international telecommunications.

All this astonishing and very rapid development has changed the lives of almost everyone.

But in spite of all the progress that has been made the greatest problem in the world today remains the gap between rich and poor countries, and we shall not begin to close this gap until we hear less about nationalism and more about interdependence.

One of the main aims of the Commonwealth is to make an effective contribution towards redressing the economic balance between nations.

Yet in spite of these advances the age-old problems of human communication are still with us. We have the means of sending and receiving messages, we can travel to meetings in distant parts of the world, we can exchange experts; but we still have difficulty in finding the right messages to send, we can still ignore the messages we don't like to hear, and we can still talk in riddles and listen without trying to comprehend.

Perhaps even more serious is the risk that this mastery of technology may blind us to the more fundamental needs of people. Electronics cannot create comradeship; computers cannot generate compassion; satellites cannot transmit tolerance.

And no amount of technology could have engineered the spirit of the Commonwealth that was so evident in Delhi or the frank, friendly and understanding communication that such a spirit makes possible.

25 December 1984

The 1984 Christmas broadcast featured footage of the christening of Prince Harry, who was born that year. In her message the Queen spoke about the lessons adults can learn from children.

The happy arrival of our fourth grandchild gave great cause for family celebrations. But for parents and grandparents, a birth is also a time for reflection on what the future holds for the baby and how they can best ensure its safety and happiness.

To do that, I believe we must be prepared to learn as much from them as they do from us. We could use some of that sturdy confidence and devastating honesty with which children rescue us from self-doubts and self-delusions. We could borrow that unstinting trust of the child in its parents for our dealings with each other.

Above all, we must retain the child's readiness to forgive, with which we are all born and which it is all too easy to lose as we grow older. Without it, divisions between families, communities and nations remain unbridgeable. We owe it to our children and grandchildren to live up to the standards of behaviour and tolerance which we are so eager to teach them.

EVERY INVESTITURE BRINGS STORIES OF BRAVERY AND SELF-SACRIFICE. THESE SUCCESS STORIES ARE OFTEN PUSHED INTO THE BACKGROUND BUT THEY ARE THE GUARANTEE OF OUR FUTURE.

QUEEN ELIZABETH II

25 December 1985

The year 1985 saw multiple lethal disasters, including an earthquake in Mexico, a volcanic eruption in Columbia, famine in Africa, and a plane crash off the coast of Ireland. The Queen's Christmas message focused on the good news stories of the year, in particular praising remarkable public achievements.

Looking at the morning newspapers, listening to the radio and watching television, it is only too easy to conclude that nothing is going right in the world.

All this year we seem to have had nothing but bad news with a constant stream of reports of plane crashes, earthquakes, volcanic eruptions and famine – and as if natural disasters were not enough, we hear of riots, wars, acts of terrorism and generally of man's inhumanity to man.

It used to be said that 'no news is good news' but today you might well think that 'good news is no news'.

Yet there is a lot of good news and some wonderful things are going on in spite of the frightening headlines. Just think of the quiet courage and dedication of the peace-keepers and the rescue workers and all those who work so hard to restore shattered lives and disrupted communities.

I am in the fortunate position of being able to meet many of these people, for every year some two thousand come to Investitures at Buckingham Palace to be honoured for acts of bravery or to be recognised for service to their fellow citizens.

They come from all walks of life and they don't blow their own trumpets; so unless, like me, you are able to read the citations describing what they have done, you could not begin to guess at some of the remarkable stories that lie behind their visits to the Palace.

Every Investiture brings stories of bravery and self-sacrifice.

These success stories are often pushed into the background but they are the guarantee of our future.

Christmas is a time of good news. I believe it is a time to look at the good things in life and to remember that there are a great many people trying to make the world a better place, even though their efforts may go unrecognised.

There is a lesson in this for us all and we should never forget our obligation to make our own individual contributions, however small, towards the sum of human goodness.

25 December 1986

In her 1986 Christmas message, The Queen spoke about society's responsibility towards children. The broadcast included footage filmed in a stable of the Royal Mews at Buckingham Palace.

Christmas is a festival for all Christians, but it is particularly a festival for children. As we all know, it commemorates the birth of a child, who was born to ordinary people, and who grew up very simply in his own small home town and was trained to be a carpenter.

The infant Jesus was fortunate in one very important respect. His parents were loving and considerate. They did their utmost to protect him from harm. They left their own home and became refugees, to save him from King Herod, and they brought him up according to the traditions of their faith.

On this birthday festival, which we try to make an occasion of happiness, we must not forget that there are some children who are victims of ill treatment and neglect.

It is no easy task to care for and bring up children, whatever your circumstances – whether you are famous or quite unknown. But we could all help by letting the spirit of Christmas fill our homes with love and care and by heeding Our Lord's injunction to treat others as you would like them to treat you.

25 December 1987

In a year that saw a terrorist bombing kill 11 people in Enniskillen in County Fermanagh, Northern Ireland, the Queen's Christmas message focused on tolerance and forgiveness.

Like everyone else, I learn about what is going on in the world from the media, but I am fortunate to have another source of information. Every day hundreds of letters come to my desk, and I make a point of reading as many of them as I possibly can.

The vast majority are a pleasure to read. There are also sad ones from people who want help, there are interesting ones from people who want to tell me what they think about current issues, or who have suggestions to make about changing the way things are done. Others are full of frank advice for me and my family and some of them do not hesitate to be critical.

I value all these letters for keeping me in touch with your views and opinions, but there are a few letters which reflect the darker side of human nature.

It is only too easy for passionate loyalty to one's own country, race or religion, or even to one's favourite football club, to be corroded into intolerance, bigotry and ultimately into violence.

We have witnessed some frightening examples of this in recent years. All too often intolerance creates the resentment and anger which fill the headlines and divide communities and nations and even families.

From time to time we also see some inspiring examples of tolerance. Mr Gordon Wilson, whose daughter Marie lost her life in the horrifying explosion at Enniskillen on Remembrance Sunday, impressed the whole world by the depth of his forgiveness.

His strength, and that of his wife, and the courage of their daughter, came from their Christian conviction. All of us will echo their prayer that out of the personal tragedies of Enniskillen may come a reconciliation between the communities.

Of course it is right that people should hold their beliefs and their faiths strongly and sincerely, but perhaps we should also have the humility to accept that, while we each have a right to our own convictions, others have a right to theirs too.

9 May 1988

On 9 May 1988, the Queen gave a speech at the opening of the new Parliament House in Canberra to mark the bicentenary of Australia.

In this bicentenary year, Australians are looking back over the events of the last two hundred years. This is well worth while because the events link together to tell a story of remarkable achievement.

This is a special occasion for the Parliament, but it is also a very important day for all the people of Australia. After 87 years of Federation, a permanent home has been provided for Parliament, which is both the living expression of that Federation and the embodiment of the democratic principles of freedom, equality and justice.

Parliamentary democracy is a compelling ideal, but it is a fragile institution. It cannot be imposed and it is only too easily destroyed. It needs the positive dedication of the people as a whole, and of their elected representatives, to make it work.

The earliest free settlers brought their ideals of a democratic society with them, and succeeding generations of Australians have inherited those principles and put them to work in what we know as the parliamentary system.

Commitment to parliamentary democracy lies at the heart of this nation's maturity, tolerance and humanity. This is surely one of the characteristics that has attracted so many people to come to Australia from countries which do not enjoy the benefits of the parliamentary system in such large measure.

This new Parliament House will become the work place for the men and wome into whose hands Australians choose to place legislative and executive responsibility. The chambers will become the centres for debate on all the pressing issues of government, and future generations of Australians will look to those who work here for national security, wise legislation and fair administration.

More than ten thousand men and women can take great pride in the parts they have played in the creation of this symbol of Australian unity and democracy.

MORE THAN TEN
THOUSAND MEN
AND WOMEN CAN
TAKE GREAT PRIDE
IN THE PARTS THEY
HAVE PLAYED IN
THE CREATION OF
THIS SYMBOL OF
AUSTRALIAN UNITY
AND DEMOCRACY.

QUEEN ELIZABETH II

Unlike all the other planets in the solar system, Earth shimmers green and blue in the sunlight and looks a very pleasant place to live.

QUEEN ELIZABETH II

25 December 1989

In her 1989 Christmas message, the Queen urged children to respect and protect their world, in light of global concern about environmental damage. The broadcast featured footage from a Save the Children Fund children's concert in the Royal Albert Hall.

Quite a lot of you have written to me during the last year or so, saying how worried you are about the future of our planet.

Many of you will have heard of the greenhouse effect, and perhaps you've heard too about even more urgent problems caused by the pollution of our rivers and seas and the cutting down of the great forests. These problems don't affect just the countries where they are happening and they make neighbourly co-operation throughout the world a pressing necessity.

With all your lives before you, I am sure that you take an optimistic view of the future. But it is already too late to prevent all forms of damage to the natural world. Some species of wild plants and animals are, sadly, bound to become extinct. But the great thing to remember is that it is not too late to reduce the damage if we change attitudes and behaviour.

You've all seen pictures of the earth taken from space. Unlike all the other planets in the solar system, earth shimmers green and blue in the sunlight and looks a very pleasant place to live.

These pictures should remind us that the future of all life on earth depends on how we behave towards one another, and how we treat the plants and the animals that share our world with us.

You children have something to give us which is priceless. You can still look at the world with a sense of wonder and remind us grown-ups that life is wonderful and precious. Often a child's helplessness and vulnerability bring out the best in us.

Part of that 'best in us' could be a particular tenderness towards this earth which we share as human beings, all of us, and, together, as the nations of the world, will leave to our children and our children's children. We must be kind to it for their sake.

HORRIBLE, YET HOPEFUL

YET

HOPEFUL

1990–1999

The 1990s were turbulent times, both for the Royal family and international relations. In 1991 the Queen made her first and only wartime broadcast of her reign when British troops engaged in war in the Gulf. She was also in the global spotlight when she gave her iconic address to the US Congress, and with her first ever state visit to Russia to meet newly elected President Yeltsin. The unfortunate events of 1992 could not escape mention in her famous 'Annus Horribilis' speech, and after the death of Princess Diana in 1997 she addressed a nation in mourning in a moving tribute. In spite of all this turmoil, the Queen did have occasion to speak in celebration of some happy events – the 50th anniversary of the end of the Second World War and her and Prince Philip's Golden Wedding anniversary. She ended the decade and the millennium with a message of hope for the future.

25 December 1990

In her 1990 Christmas message, with war brewing in the Arabian Gulf, the Queen paid tribute to the role of the armed services.

It seems to me that there is one deep and overriding anxiety for us all on which we should reflect today. That is the threat of war in the Middle East.

The servicemen in the Gulf who are spending Christmas at their posts under this threat are much in our thoughts. And there are many others, at home and abroad, servicemen and civilians, who are away from their own firesides. Wherever they are, may they all, when their duty is done, soon be reunited with their families safe and sound.

At the same time we must remember those still held hostage. Some of them have spent years in captivity, and Christmas must, for them, be especially hard to bear. My heart goes out to them and to their families.

We can, at least, rejoice at the safe return of many of their compatriots over the last weeks, and salute the courage which they have shown.

Wars, threats of wars and civil disturbance inevitably cause thousands of innocent people to become refugees and to have their lives ruined or disrupted. It is difficult for us, safe at home, to contemplate the scale of the suffering for homeless and hungry people caused by the ever-widening consequences of the crisis in the Gulf.

The invasion of Kuwait was an example on an international scale of an evil which has beset us at different levels in recent years – attempts by ruthless people to impose their will on the peaceable majority.

I, like many others, was much heartened by the virtually unanimous opposition of the international community to the unprovoked invasion of Kuwait, and by the speed with which moves were made to try to relieve the plight of the innocent victims.

I want, therefore, to say thank you today to the men and women who, day in and day out, carry on their daily life in difficult and dangerous circumstances. By just getting on with the job, they are getting the better of those who want to harm our way of life.

Let us think of them this Christmas, wherever they are in the world, and pray that their resolution remains undiminished.

24 February 1991

On 24 February 1991, the Queen made the only wartime broadcast of her reign, in which she prayed for her soldiers deployed to the Persian Gulf as part of Operation Desert Storm.

As a nation, we are rightly proud of our Armed Forces. That pride has been fully justified by their conduct in the Gulf War so far. As they, with our allies, face a fresh and yet sterner challenge, I hope that we can unite, and pray that their success will be as swift as it is certain and that it may be achieved with as small a cost in human life and suffering as possible. Then may the true reward of their courage be granted – a just and lasting peace.

16 May 1991

During a 13-day visit to the United States, the Queen addressed a joint meeting of Congress, to rapturous applause. She spoke of the spirit of democracy shared by the two countries and of their role in continuing to strive for their common values.

The concept so simply described by Abraham Lincoln as government by the people, of the people, for the people is fundamental to our two nations. Your Congress and our Parliament are the twin pillars of our civilisations, and the chief among the many treasures that we have inherited from our predecessors. We, like you, are staunch believers in the freedom of the individual and the rule of a fair and just law. These principles are shared with our European partners, and with the wider Atlantic community. They are the bedrock of the Western world.

Some people believe that power grows from the barrel of a gun. So it can, but history shows that it never grows well, nor for very long. Force, in the end, is sterile. We have gone a better way. Our societies rest on mutual agreement, on contract and on consensus. A significant part of your social contract is written down in your Constitution. Ours rests on custom and will. The spirit behind both, however, is precisely the same; it is the spirit of democracy. These ideals are clear enough, but they must never be taken for granted. They have to be protected and nurtured through every change and fluctuation.

I want to take this opportunity to express the gratitude of the British people to the people of the United States of America for their steadfast loyalty to our common enterprise throughout this turbulent century. The future is, as ever, obscure. The only certainty is that it'll present the world with new and daunting problems, but if we continue to stick to our fundamental ideals, I have every confidence that we can resolve them. Recent events in the Gulf have proved that it is possible to do just that.

The swift and dramatic changes in Eastern Europe in the last decade have opened up great opportunities for the people of those countries. They are finding their own paths to freedom. But the paths would have been blocked if the Atlantic Alliance had not stood together, if your country and mine had not stood together. Let us never forget that lesson.

IF SHE HADN'T BEEN BORN INTO ROYALTY, I THINK SHE MIGHT HAVE MADE IT ON HER OWN AS A DISTINGUISHED POLITICIAN OR DIPLOMAT.

BILL CLINTON
AFTER THE QUEEN'S DEATH, SEPTEMBER 2022

Britain is at the heart of a growing movement towards greater cohesion within Europe and within the European community in particular. This is going to mean radical economic, social and political evolution. NATO, too, is adapting to the new realities in Eastern Europe and the Soviet Union and to changing attitudes in the West. It is Britain's prime concern to ensure that the new Europe is open and liberal and that it works in growing harmony with the United States and the other members of the Atlantic community. All our history in this and earlier centuries underlines the basic point that the best progress is made when Europeans and Americans act in concert.

We must not allow ourselves to be enticed into a form of continental insularity. I believe this is particularly important now at a time of major social, environmental and economic changes in your continent, and in Asia and Africa. We must make sure that those changes do not become convulsions, for the primary interest of our societies is not domination but stability. Stability, so that ordinary men and women everywhere can get on with their lives in confidence. Our two countries have a special advantage in seeking to guide the process of change because of the rich ethnic and cultural diversity of both our societies. Stability in our own countries depends on tolerance and understanding between different communities. Perhaps we can together build on our experience to spread the message we have learned at home to those regions where it has yet to be absorbed. Whether we will be able to realise our hopes will depend on the maintenance of an acceptable degree of international order. In this we see the United Nations as the essential instrument in the promotion of peace and co-operation. We look to its charter as the guardian of civilised conduct between nations.

In 1941, President Roosevelt spoke of freedom of speech and expression everywhere in the world, freedom of every person to worship God in their own way everywhere in the world, freedom from want and freedom from fear. Just as our societies have prospered through their reliance on contract, not force, so too will the world be a better place for the spread of their mutual respect and good faith, which are so fundamental to our way of life. Freedom under the rule of law is an international as well as a national concern. That thought might be in the mind of those of you attending the 50th anniversary meeting of the British American Parliamentary Group in July. Both our houses are eager to greet you. They will, I know, tell you that our aim as Britons and Europeans is to celebrate and nurture our longstanding friendship with the people of the United States. We want to build on that foundation and to do better. And if the going gets rough, I hope you can still agree with your poet Emmerson, who wrote in 1847, 'I feel in regard to this aged England ... with a kind of instinct that she sees a little better on a cloudy day, and that, in storm of battle or calamity, she has a secret vigour and a pulse like a cannon.' You will find us worthy partners. And we are proud to have you as our friends. May God bless America.

25 December 1991

In the year that Boris Yeltsin won the first public elections in Russia, the Queen's Christmas message focused on the changes taking place across Eastern Europe and Russia, and the importance of democratic traditions.

In 1952, when I first broadcast to you at Christmas, the world was a very different place to the one we live in today.

Only seven years had passed since the end of the most destructive wars in the history of mankind. Even the end of the hostilities did not bring the true peace for which so many had fought and died. What became known as the 'Cold War' sustained an atmosphere of suspicion, anxiety and fear for many years.

Then, quite suddenly, everything began to change, and the changes have happened with bewildering speed. In 1989 the Berlin Wall came down. Since then the rest of the world has watched, fascinated, as oppressive regimes have crumbled under popular pressure.

One by one, these liberated peoples have taken the first hesitant, and sometimes painful, steps towards open and democratic societies.

Naturally, we welcome this, and it may be that we can help them achieve their aims. But, in doing that, we need to remind ourselves of the essential elements which form the bedrock of our own free way of life – so highly valued and so easily taken for granted.

This can be an opportunity to reflect on our good fortune, and on whether we have anything to offer by way of example to those who have recently broken free of dictatorship. We, who claim to be of the free world, should examine what we really mean by freedom, and how we can help to ensure that, once in place, it is there to stay.

There are all sorts of elements to a free society, but I believe that among the most important is the willingness of ordinary men and women to play a part in the life of their community, rather than confining themselves to their own narrow interests.

The peoples of the former Soviet Union and Eastern Europe have broken the mould of autocracy. I hope that we will be able to help them as they learn that the democracy which has replaced it depends, not on political structures, but on the goodwill and the sense of responsibility of each and every citizen.

24 November 1992

On the 40th anniversary of her accession, the Queen gave a speech at Guildhall to mark the occasion, in which she referred to recent events as part of an 'Annus horribilis'.

1992 is not a year on which I shall look back with undiluted pleasure. In the words of one of my more sympathetic correspondents, it has turned out to be an 'Annus Horribilis'. I suspect that I am not alone in thinking it so. Indeed, I suspect that there are very few people or institutions unaffected by these last months of worldwide turmoil and uncertainty. This generosity and wholehearted kindness of the Corporation of the City to Prince Philip and me would be welcome at any time, but at this particular moment, in the aftermath of Friday's tragic fire at Windsor, it is especially so.

And, after this last weekend, we appreciate all the more what has been set before us today. Years of experience, however, have made us a bit more canny than the lady, less well versed than us in the splendours of City hospitality, who, when she was offered a balloon glass for her brandy, asked for 'only half a glass, please'.

It is possible to have too much of a good thing. A well-meaning bishop was obviously doing his best when he told Queen Victoria, 'Ma'am, we cannot pray too often, nor too fervently, for the Royal Family'. The Queen's reply was: 'Too fervently, no; too often, yes'. I, like Queen Victoria, have always been a believer in that old maxim 'moderation in all things'.

I sometimes wonder how future generations will judge the events of this tumultuous year. I dare say that history will take a slightly more moderate view than that of some contemporary commentators. Distance is well-known to lend enchantment, even to the less attractive views. After all, it has the inestimable advantage of hindsight.

But it can also lend an extra dimension to judgement, giving it a leavening of moderation and compassion – even of wisdom – that is sometimes lacking in the reactions of those whose task it is in life to offer instant opinions on all things great and small.

No section of the community has all the virtues, neither does any have all the vices. I am quite sure that most people try to do their jobs as best they can, even if the result is not always entirely successful. He who has never failed to reach perfection has a right to be the harshest critic.

1992 IS NOT A YEAR ON WHICH I SHALL LOOK BACK WITH UNDILUTED PLEASURE. IN THE WORDS OF ONE OF MY MORE SYMPATHETIC CORRESPONDENTS, IT HAS TURNED OUT TO BE AN 'ANNUS HORRIBILIS'.

QUEEN ELIZABETH II

There can be no doubt, of course, that criticism is good for people and institutions that are part of public life. No institution – City, Monarchy, whatever – should expect to be free from the scrutiny of those who give it their loyalty and support, not to mention those who don't.

But we are all part of the same fabric of our national society and that scrutiny, by one part of another, can be just as effective if it is made with a touch of gentleness, good humour and understanding.

This sort of questioning can also act, and it should do so, as an effective engine for change.

Forty years is quite a long time. I am glad to have had the chance to witness, and to take part in, many dramatic changes in life in this country. But I am glad to say that the magnificent standard of hospitality given on so many occasions to the Sovereign by the Lord Mayor of London has not changed at all.

25 December 1993

The Queen spoke in her 1993 Christmas message about volunteers, praising their achievements in working for peace and the relief of others.

All too often ... we find ourselves watching or listening to the sort of news which, as a daily diet, can be almost overwhelming. It makes us yearn for some good news.

If we can look on the bright side, so much the better, but that does not mean we should shield ourselves from the truth, even if it is unwelcome. I believe that we should be aware of events which, in the old days, might have passed us by. But that means facing up to the question of what we can do to use that awareness for the greater good.

The simple answer is, of course, all too little. But there is another answer. It is that the more we know, the more we feel responsible, and the more we want to help.

Those involved in international charity work confirm that modern communications have helped to bring them public support and made them more effective. People are not shunning the added responsibility, but shouldering it.

All of us owe a debt to those volunteers who are out there in the front line, putting our donations to use by looking after the wounded, the hungry and the oppressed. Much of their work never reaches the headlines or television screens, but their example should inspire us all the same.

25 December 1994

The Queen's Christmas message in 1994 reflected on past and present peace efforts, in a year which saw the 50th anniversary of the D-Day landings and the first ever state visit to Russia.

As Prince Philip and I stood watching the British veterans march past on the beach at Arromanches, my own memories of 1944 were stirred – of how it was to wait anxiously for news of friends and relations engaged in that massive and hazardous operation; of the subsequent ebb and flow of the battles in France and then in Germany itself; and of the gradual realisation that the war really was at least coming to an end.

Since those D-Day commemorations, Prince Philip and I have been to Russia. While we were in St Petersburg, we had the opportunity to honour the millions of patriotic Russians who died fighting the common enemy.

To see British and Russian veterans standing together, in memory of the sacrifices of their comrades-in-arms, was a moving experience.

I never thought it would be possible in my lifetime to join with the Patriarch of Moscow and his congregation in a service in that wonderful cathedral in the heart of the Moscow Kremlin.

We are frequently reminded, of course, that violence and hatred are still all too much in evidence. We can take some comfort, however, from the fact that more people throughout the world, year by year, have real hope of their children growing up in peace and free from fear.

Christ taught us to love our enemies and to do good to them that hate us. It is a hard lesson to learn, but this year we have seen shining examples of that generosity of spirit which alone can banish division and prejudice.

What is it that makes people turn from violence, and try to bring peace to their community? Most of all, I believe, it is their determination to bring reality to their hopes of a better world for their children.

If we resolve to be considerate and to help our neighbours; to make friends with people of different races and religions; and, as our Lord said, to look to our own faults before we criticise others, we will be keeping faith with those who landed in Normandy and fought so doggedly for their belief in freedom, peace and human decency.

25 December 1995

In 1995, the 50th anniversary of the end of Second World War saw celebrations across Britain. The Queen visited South Africa for the first time since 1947 and met President Nelson Mandela. That year her Christmas message focused on the role of ordinary men and women in bringing about peace.

During a year of wartime commemorations which has seen Commonwealth countries honouring their past, it has sometimes been tempting to let nostalgia lend a rosy glow to memories of war, and to forget the benefits of the relatively peaceful years bought for us by the heroism and sacrifice to which we have been paying tribute.

Those who suffered the horrors of warfare, in whatever guise, will not have been prey to this temptation. For them, war was not a 'Boys' Own' tale of comradeship and good cheer, but one of hard slog, danger, suffering and exhaustion.

Those songs we sang during the VE Day commemorations did much to brighten the days of war, and they certainly cheered us last May. But, as any veteran will tell you, there was a lot more to the war years than dreaming of the White Cliffs of Dover.

In talking to the veterans, I was forcibly reminded of the detachment with which those personally unaffected by violence can view its effect on others.

We heard much, in May and August this year, of how the future of the free world was saved by the ordinary men and women who did their bit for the victory of 1945.

It is the ordinary men and women who, so often, have done more than anyone else to bring peace to troubled lands. It is they who suffer most, and it is up to others to see that their courage and common sense are rewarded. It should not be too much to ask.

During my visit to South Africa last March, I was able to see, in a township, how the energy and inspiration of one person could benefit thousands of others. And that one person would lay no claim to be anything other than ordinary – whatever you or I might think of her!

25 December 1996

In 1996, the Queen went to Poland, the Czech Republic and Thailand. Two terrible massacres had shocked the world that year: a shooting in a school in Dunblane and an attack in Port Arthur, Tasmania. In her Christmas message, the Queen spoke on the theme of hope for the future.

So, the past, with its traditions, has its lessons for us in 1996. And this year, in our travels, Prince Philip and I have also been looking to the future. I and all my family have always felt that one of our most important duties is to express, in our visits overseas, the goodwill of our country towards friends abroad, near and far.

So, last spring, we visited Poland and the Czech Republic, where we saw the development of democracy and prosperity in countries which only recently were communist-governed. And everywhere we received the best of welcomes. In the autumn we went to Thailand, where we renewed old friendships and witnessed the blending of tradition with a dynamic commercial spirit.

There was also a happy visit to this country by the President of France. And I shall never forget the State Visit of President Mandela. The most gracious of men has shown us all how to accept the facts of the past without bitterness, how to see new opportunities as more important than old disputes, and how to look forward with courage and optimism.

His example is a continuing inspiration to the whole Commonwealth and to all those everywhere who work for peace and reconciliation.

This, I know, has been a difficult year for many families. Discord, sickness, bereavement, even tragedy have touched all too many lives. We recall, with sadness and bewilderment, the horror of Dunblane and Port Arthur. We watch anxiously as violence threatens again to disrupt the lives of the people of Northern Ireland.

In difficult times, it is tempting for all of us, especially those who suffer, to look back and say 'if only'. But to look back in that way is to look down a blind alley. Better to look forward and say 'if only'.

5 September 1997

On 31 August 1997, Princess Diana died in a tragic car accident in Paris. On the eve of her funeral, the Queen gave a speech paying tribute to Diana and giving thanks to all those who came to pay their respects.

Since last Sunday's dreadful news we have seen, throughout Britain and around the world, an overwhelming expression of sadness at Diana's death.

We have all been trying in our different ways to cope. It is not easy to express a sense of loss, since the initial shock is often succeeded by a mixture of other feelings: disbelief, incomprehension, anger – and concern for those who remain. We have all felt those emotions in these last few days. So what I say to you now, as your Queen and as a grandmother, I say from my heart.

First, I want to pay tribute to Diana myself. She was an exceptional and gifted human being. In good times and bad, she never lost her capacity to smile and laugh, nor to inspire others with her warmth and kindness. I admired and respected her – for her energy and commitment to others, and especially for her devotion to her two boys. This week at Balmoral, we have all been trying to help William and Harry come to terms with the devastating loss that they and the rest of us have suffered.

No one who knew Diana will ever forget her. Millions of others who never met her, but felt they knew her, will remember her. I for one believe there are lessons to be drawn from her life and from the extraordinary and moving reaction to her death. I share in your determination to cherish her memory.

This is also an opportunity for me, on behalf of my family, and especially Prince Charles and William and Harry, to thank all of you who have brought flowers, sent messages and paid your respects in so many ways to a remarkable person. These acts of kindness have been a huge source of help and comfort.

Our thoughts are also with Diana's family and the families of those who died with her. I know that they too have drawn strength from what has happened since last weekend, as they seek to heal their sorrow and then to face the future without a loved one.

I hope that tomorrow we can all, wherever we are, join in expressing our grief at Diana's loss, and gratitude for her all-too-short life. It is a chance to show to the whole world the British nation united in grief and respect.

May those who died rest in peace and may we, each and every one of us, thank God for someone who made many, many people happy.

20 November 1997

The Queen and Prince Philip celebrated their Golden Wedding anniversary on 20 November 1997 at a lunch at Banqueting House in London, where the Queen made a speech looking back on their fifty years of marriage.

When Prince Philip and I were married on this day fifty years ago, Britain had just endured six years of war, emerging battered but victorious. Prince Philip had served in the Royal Navy in the Far East, while I was grappling, in the ATS, with the complexities of the combustion engine and learning to drive an ambulance with care.

Today, Prime Minister, we accept your generous hospitality in a very different Britain. The Cold War is over and our country is at peace. The economy in your charge, and which you inherited, is soundly based and growing. And, during these last fifty years, the mass-media culture has transformed our lives in any number of ways, allowing us to learn more about our fellow human beings than, in 1947, we would have thought possible.

What a remarkable fifty years they have been: for the world, for the Commonwealth and for Britain.

This, too, is an opportunity for Prince Philip and me to offer, in the words of one of the most beautiful prayers in the English language, our 'humble and hearty thanks' to all those in Britain and around the world who have welcomed us and sustained us and our family, in the good times and the bad, so unstintingly over many years.

All too often, I fear, Prince Philip has had to listen to me speaking. Frequently we have discussed my intended speech beforehand and, as you will imagine, his views have been expressed in a forthright manner.

He is someone who doesn't take easily to compliments but he has, quite simply, been my strength and stay all these years, and I, and his whole family, and this and many other countries, owe him a debt greater than he would ever claim, or we shall ever know.

He is someone who doesn't take easily to compliments but he has, quite simply, been my strength and stay all these years.

QUEEN ELIZABETH II

THOUGH WE EACH
LEAD DIFFERENT LIVES,
THE EXPERIENCE OF
GROWING OLDER,
AND THE JOYS AND
EMOTIONS WHICH IT
BRINGS, ARE FAMILIAR
TO US ALL.

QUEEN ELIZABETH II

25 December 1998

In 1998 the Queen spoke in her Christmas message about the lessons to be learned by different generations from each other. The broadcast featured footage of Queen Elizabeth and the Queen Mother visiting the Field of Remembrance at Westminster Abbey, the Queen at Ypres and in Paris, and the reception for the Prince of Wales's 50th birthday.

It is not always easy for those in their teens or twenties to believe that someone of my age – of the older generation – might have something useful to say to them. But I would say that my mother has much to say to me.

Indeed, her vigour and enjoyment of life is a great example of how to close the so-called generation gap. She has an extraordinary capacity to bring happiness into other people's lives. And her own vitality and warmth is returned to her by those whom she meets.

But there are many of my mother's generation still with us. They can remember the First World War. Prince Philip and I can recall only the Second.

Memories such as these are a consequence of age, and not a virtue in themselves. But with age does come experience and that can be a virtue if it is sensibly used. Though we each lead different lives, the experience of growing older, and the joys and emotions which it brings, are familiar to us all.

We parents and grandparents must learn to trust our children and grandchildren as they seize their opportunities, but we can, at the same time, caution and comfort if things go wrong, or guide and explain if we are needed.

My own grandchildren and their generation have a remarkable grasp of modern technology. They are lucky to have the freedom to travel and learn about foreign cultures at an age when the appetite for learning is keen. I see them pushing out the boundaries of science, sport and music, of drama and discovery.

Last June Prince Philip and I gave a party for 900 of Britain's Young Achievers. Buckingham Palace was brimming with young people who, in their short lives, have already set an example to us all: they are living proof that the timeless virtues of honesty, integrity, initiative and compassion are just as important today as they have ever been.

25 December 1999

The Queen's Christmas message of 1999 was the last of the millennium. She reflected on the lessons of history and looked to the future. It was filmed in the White Drawing Room of Windsor Castle and included footage of a reception for Young Achievers at the Palace of Holyroodhouse, and a reception for members of the emergency services at Buckingham Palace.

This December we are looking back not just on one year, but on a hundred years and a thousand years. History is measured in centuries. More than ever we are aware of being a tiny part of the infinite sweep of time when we move from one century and one millennium to another.

And as I look to the future I have no doubt at all that the one certainty is change – and the pace of that change will only seem to increase.

The Commonwealth, as with the process of devolution in the United Kingdom, reminds us of the importance of bringing the lessons of the past to bear on the aspirations for a better future.

To do this we need to draw from our history those constant and unchanging values which have stood the test of time and experience. Fairness and compassion, justice and tolerance; these are the landmarks from the past which can guide us through the years ahead.

These timeless values tell us above all about the way we should relate to people rather than to things; thinking of others, not just of ourselves.

The future is not only about new gadgets, modern technology or the latest fashion, important as these may be. At the centre of our lives – today and tomorrow – must be the message of caring for others, the message at the heart of Christianity and of all the great religions.

This message – love thy neighbour as thyself – may be for Christians 2,000 years old. But it is as relevant today as it ever was. I believe it gives us the guidance and the reassurance we need as we step over the threshold into the 21st century.

And I for one am looking forward to this new Millennium.

THIS DECEMBER
WE ARE LOOKING
BACK NOT JUST ON
ONE YEAR, BUT ON A
HUNDRED YEARS AND
A THOUSAND YEARS.

QUEEN ELIZABETH II

MEMORABLE MILESTONES

MILESTONES

2000–2009

The Queen spoke on the occasion of many important milestones during her reign, and this decade was no exception. In March 2000 she gave a speech at the Sydney Opera House, following a referendum in which Australia decided to retain the Queen as Head of State, and in 2004, she gave an address at a state banquet in Paris celebrating 100 years of entente cordiale. The 2000s saw their fair share of tragedy, with the 9/11 and July 2005 terror attacks, the Boxing Day tsunami and the war in Afghanistan, events which the Queen spoke of with her customary sensitivity. Themes running through her Christmas messages included the importance of fostering understanding between faiths and generations, helping the disadvantaged and of selfless acts. There were occasions that called for sombre words of reflection, such as the death of the Queen Mother, and others that called for messages of celebration, such as the Golden Jubilee and the Queen's 80th birthday.

20 March 2000

In November 1999, a referendum was held in Australia, in which the majority voted to retain the Queen as Head of State. In the first speech of a tour of the nation, the Queen reflected on the referendum.

In January next year Australia will mark the centenary of Federation and one hundred years of nationhood. It will be a time of justified celebration, but I hope it will also be a time of pause and quiet reflection.

At that time I shall reflect – perhaps with that hint of surprise which comes with age – that my formal commitment to Australia will have spanned almost precisely half of this country's life as a federated nation.

You can understand therefore that it was with the closest interest that I followed the debate leading up to the referendum held last year on the proposal to amend the Constitution.

I have always made it clear that the future of the Monarchy in Australia is an issue for you, the Australian people, and you alone to decide by democratic and constitutional means. It should not be otherwise.

As I said at the time, I respect and accept the outcome of the referendum. In the light of the result last November, I shall continue faithfully to serve as Queen of Australia under the Constitution to the very best of my ability, as I have tried to do for these past 48 years. It is my duty to seek to remain true to the interests of Australia and all Australians as we enter the 21st century.

That is my duty. It is also my privilege and my pleasure. I cannot forget that I was on my way to Australia when my father died. Since then and since I first stepped ashore here in Sydney in February 1954 I have felt part of this rugged, honest, creative land. I have shared in the joys and the sorrows, the challenges and the changes that have shaped this country's history over these past fifty years.

But we must look forward as well as back. Australia has always been a country on the move and will go on being so – it is not for nothing that the anthem is 'Advance Australia Fair'.

Whatever the future may bring, my lasting respect and deep affection for Australia and Australians everywhere will remain as strong as ever. That is what I have come here to say; that is why I am pleased to be back; and that is why I am looking forward to these next two weeks among you in this great country.

IT IS MY DUTY TO SEEK TO REMAIN TRUE TO THE INTERESTS OF AUSTRALIA AND ALL AUSTRALIANS AS WE ENTER THE 21ST CENTURY.

QUEEN ELIZABETH II

25 December 2001

In her 50th Christmas message, the Queen spoke of the importance of communities working together to respond to problems and disasters. That year the 9/11 terrorist attacks in New York had killed around 3,000 people and there was an outbreak of foot-and-mouth disease in the UK and a famine in Sudan.

For many people all over the world, the year 2001 seems to have brought them more than their fair share of trials and disasters.

The terrorist outrages in the United States last September brought home to us the pain and grief of ordinary people the world over who find themselves innocently caught up in such evil.

During the following days we struggled to find ways of expressing our horror at what had happened. In these circumstances so many of us, whatever our religion, need our faith more than ever to sustain and guide us. Every one of us needs to believe in the value of all that is good and honest; we need to let this belief drive and influence our actions.

All the major faiths tell us to give support and hope to others in distress. We in this country have tried to bring comfort to all those who were bereaved, or who suffered loss or injury in September's tragic events, through those moving services at St Paul's and more recently at Westminster Abbey.

On these occasions and during the countless other acts of worship during this past year, we came together as a community – of relations, friends and neighbours – to draw strength in troubled times from those around us.

I believe that strong and open communities matter both in good times as well as bad. Certainly they provide a way of helping one another. I would like to pay tribute to so many of you who work selflessly for others in your neighbourhood needing care and support.

Communities also give us an important sense of belonging, which is a compelling need in all of us. We all enjoy moments of great happiness and suffer times of profound sadness; the happiness is heightened, the sadness softened when it is shared.

But there is more than that. A sense of belonging to a group, which has in common the same desire for a fair and ordered society, helps to overcome differences and misunderstanding by reducing prejudice, ignorance and fear.

8 April 2002

On 30 March 2002, the Queen Mother passed way, aged 101. The following week the Queen gave a moving speech, paying tribute to her mother and the times she lived in and giving thanks to all those who paid their condolences.

Ever since my beloved mother died over a week ago I have been deeply moved by the outpouring of affection which has accompanied her death.

My family and I always knew what she meant for the people of this country and the special place she occupied in the hearts of so many here, in the Commonwealth and in other parts of the world. But the extent of the tribute that huge numbers of you have paid my mother in the last few days has been overwhelming. I have drawn great comfort from so many individual acts of kindness and respect.

Over the years I have met many people who have had to cope with family loss, sometimes in the most tragic of circumstances. So I count myself fortunate that my mother was blessed with a long and happy life. She had an infectious zest for living, and this remained with her until the very end. I know too that her faith was always a great strength to her.

At the ceremony tomorrow I hope that sadness will blend with a wider sense of thanksgiving, not just for her life but for the times in which she lived – a century for this country and the Commonwealth not without its trials and sorrows, but also one of extraordinary progress, full of examples of courage and service as well as fun and laughter.

This is what my mother would have understood, because it was the warmth and affection of people everywhere which inspired her resolve, dedication and enthusiasm for life.

I thank you for the support you are giving me and my family as we come to terms with her death and the void she has left in our midst. I thank you also from my heart for the love you gave her during her life and the honour you now give her in death.

May God bless you all.

I HOPE THAT THESE
CELEBRATIONS WILL
REMIND US OF OUR
SHARED HERITAGE
AND WHAT IT MEANS
TO BE A UNITED
PEOPLE, ENJOYING
THE SUPPORT OF
FAMILIES, FRIENDS
AND NEIGHBOURS
AROUND US.

QUEEN ELIZABETH II

4 June 2002

On the occasion of her Golden Jubilee, the Queen attended a lunch at Guildhall and gave a speech reflecting on the celebrations and on the past 50 years of her reign.

I am more than conscious at the moment of the importance of football. Although this weekend comes about halfway through my Jubilee year, as far as we are concerned, it bears no relation to a rest at 'half-time'.

However, I am very glad that the fiftieth anniversary of my accession is giving so many people all over this country and in the Commonwealth an excuse to celebrate and enjoy themselves.

It has been a pretty remarkable fifty years by any standards. There have been ups and downs, but anyone who can remember what things were like after those six long years of war, appreciates what immense changes have been achieved since then.

Not everyone has been able to benefit from the growth of wealth and prosperity, but it has not been for lack of political will. I think we can look back with measured pride on the history of the last fifty years.

Since the spring of this year I have travelled extensively in this country and in the Commonwealth. It has been wonderful to experience the many special events which have brought together volunteers of all ages and organisations of all kinds.

I am quite convinced that these local celebrations have helped to remind people of the value of such neighbourhood events in building a genuine community spirit.

I hope that these celebrations will remind us of our shared heritage and what it means to be a united people, enjoying the support of families, friends and neighbours around us.

Gratitude, respect and pride, these words sum up how I feel about the people of this country and the Commonwealth – and what this Golden Jubilee means to me.

25 December 2003

The 2003 Christmas message was recorded at Combermere Barracks in Windsor, the first time in the history of the broadcast that an outside location was used. Many British servicemen and women were stationed in Iraq that year. The Queen paid tribute to the professionalism of the Armed Services.

This year I am speaking to you from the Household Cavalry Barracks in Windsor because I want to draw attention to the many servicemen and women who are stationed far from home this Christmas.

I am thinking about their wives and children, and about their parents and friends. Separation at this time is especially hard to bear.

It is not just a matter of separation. The men and women of the Services continue to face serious risks and dangers as they carry out their duties. They have done this brilliantly.

I think we all have very good reasons for feeling proud of their achievements – both in war, and as they help to build a lasting peace in troublespots across the globe.

None of this can be achieved without paying a price. I know that all our thoughts at this time are with the families who are suffering the pain of bereavement. All those who have recently lost a close relative or friend will know how difficult Christmas can be.

These individual servicemen and women are our neighbours and come from our own towns and villages; from every part of the country and from every background.

The process of training within the Navy, the Army and the Air Force has moulded them together into disciplined teams.

They have learned to take responsibility and to exercise judgement and restraint in situations of acute stress and danger. They have brought great credit to themselves and to our country as a whole.

I had an opportunity recently at the Barracks to meet some of those who played their part with such distinction in the Iraq operations. I was left with a deep sense of respect and admiration for their steadfast loyalty to each other and to our nation.

I believe there is a lesson for us all here. It is that each of us can achieve much more if we work together as members of a team.

5 April 2004

At a state banquet in Paris celebrating the centenary of the Entente Cordiale agreement, the Queen gave a speech reflecting on past relations between Britain and France.

I believe that we mark this week a most significant anniversary for our two nations. If I may be allowed tonight one small British understatement, our historical relationship has not always been smooth. For centuries we fought each other fiercely, often and everywhere – from Hastings to Waterloo, from the heights of Abraham to the mouth of the Nile.

But since 1815 our two nations have not been to war. On the contrary we have stood together, resolute in defence of liberty and democracy, notably through the terrible global conflicts of the 20th century.

This was far from inevitable when we reflect on how close we came to war over our colonies at the end of the 19th century. That we turned away from conflict to the path of partnership was due to the single-minded efforts of a small number of enlightened individuals dedicated to Franco-British rapprochement. Their immense achievement was the Entente Cordiale signed one hundred years ago this week.

I am proud of the part my great-grandfather, King Edward VII, played in this historic agreement. It was his initiative, and that of your President Loubert, to insist on reciprocal State Visits in 1903 which did so much to create the popular atmosphere for the successful political negotiations to settle our colonial disagreements the following year.

I hope that this State Visit, and the season of Entente Cordiale celebrations closing with your visit to London, Mr President, in the autumn, will likewise contribute to a new era of Franco-British partnership. Our circumstances a century on are perhaps not entirely dissimilar.

For just as our statesmen and my great-grandfather realised a hundred years ago, we too need to recognise that we cannot let immediate political pressures, however strongly felt on both sides, stand between us in the longer term. We are both reminded that neither of our two great nations, nor Europe, nor the wider Western Alliance, can afford the luxury of short-term division or discord, in the face of threats to our security and prosperity that now challenge us all.

... A CONSTANT
PRESENCE AND A
SOURCE OF WISDOM
FOR THE LEADERS OF
OUR TWO COUNTRIES...
THE GOLDEN THREAD
THAT BINDS OUR
TWO COUNTRIES,
THE PROOF OF THE
UNWAVERING FRIENDSHIP
BETWEEN OUR NATIONS.

EMMANUEL MACRON,
PRESIDENT OF FRANCE

Of course we will never agree on everything. Life would be dull indeed, not least for the rest of the world, if we did not allow ourselves a little space to live up to our national caricatures – British pragmatism and French élan; French conceptualism and British humour; British rain and French sun; I think we should enjoy the complementarity of it all.

I believe our two peoples understand this sometimes more clearly than our governments. Thousands of British are settling, living and working in France, and thousands of French are crossing the Channel to do the same. Millions of British holidaymakers visit France each year.

We remain an island, but my arrival today by train reminds us that the Tunnel marks a profound psychological shift as well as a practical advantage for many people on both sides of the Channel.

Economically and culturally we are doing so much more together, as our companies invest both ways across the Channel, and the worlds of, for example, fashion, art and sport are increasingly interdependent.

We have perhaps yet to appreciate the longer-term consequences of these increasingly widespread human links. The centenary of the Entente Cordiale is a good moment to do so.

I hope that we can use this anniversary to recognise and celebrate all that we have in common. Britain and France are two of the great nation states of Europe – old, yes, and proud of it, but eager to embrace the new, dynamic century that is upon us.

Our histories have made us frequent rivals, but like our forbears a hundred years ago, we now need to recognise that we are natural 21st-century partners in Europe and the wider world.

Ladies and Gentlemen, I ask you to rise and drink a toast to the President and people of France, *Vive la différence, mais vive L'Entente Cordiale.*

6 June 2004

At the 60th anniversary D-Day commemoration in Arromanches, the Queen spoke of the D-Day events and paid tribute to the Canadians who served in the operation.

The invasion of France in 1944 was one of the most dramatic military operations in history. It would have been difficult enough for a single nation to plan and execute such an enterprise; for a group of allies with little previous experience in co-operation, it was a major triumph.

The operation itself was a resounding success, but it was only achieved with the sacrifice of many courageous and determined Allied servicemen, including a large number of your Canadian colleagues, who landed here with you on Juno Beach.

Britain had been directly threatened by the enemy but you came across the Atlantic from the relative security of your homeland to fight for the freedom of Europe. For Canadians, involved in the fight from its earliest months, the raid on Dieppe was a tragedy but, in retrospect, the lessons learned there proved to be life-savers for many thousands when you came to land in Normandy.

The 60th anniversary of the Normandy Landings is a moment for thanksgiving, and a moment of commemoration. Today we honour all those who gave their lives in this campaign, and all of you who fought in this great struggle. I know that present and future generations join me in thanking all Canadians who took part in this great venture.

On this anniversary day, I join all your countrymen and allies in saluting you, the heroes and veterans of a historic campaign.

THE 60TH ANNIVERSARY
OF THE NORMANDY
LANDINGS IS A MOMENT
FOR THANKSGIVING,
AND A MOMENT OF
COMMEMORATION.

QUEEN ELIZABETH II

THESE NATURAL AND HUMAN TRAGEDIES PROVIDED THE HEADLINE NEWS; THEY ALSO PROVOKED A QUITE REMARKABLE HUMANITARIAN RESPONSE.

QUEEN ELIZABETH II

25 December 2005

Following the 2004 Christmas broadcast a number of global tragedies unfolded, including the Boxing Day tsunami in Southeast Asia, hurricanes in the Caribbean, floods in New Orleans, an earthquake in Pakistan and India, and terrorist attacks in London. The Queen spoke about these events praised the work of those providing humanitarian assistance.

This Christmas my thoughts are especially with those everywhere who are grieving the loss of loved ones during what for so many has been such a terrible year.

These natural and human tragedies provided the headline news; they also provoked a quite remarkable humanitarian response. People of compassion all over the world responded with immediate practical and financial help.

There may be an instinct in all of us to help those in distress, but in many cases I believe this has been inspired by religious faith. Christianity is not the only religion to teach its followers to help others and to treat your neighbour as you would want to be treated yourself.

It has been clear that in the course of this year relief workers and financial support have come from members of every faith and from every corner of the world.

There is no doubt that the process of rebuilding these communities is far from over and there will be fresh calls on our commitment to help in the future.

Certainly the need for selflessness and generosity in the face of hardship is nothing new. The veterans of the Second World War whom we honoured last summer can tell us how so often, in moments of greatest trial, those around them seemed able to draw on some inner strength to find courage and compassion. We see this today in the way that young men and women are calmly serving our country around the world, often in great danger.

This last year has reminded us that this world is not always an easy or a safe place to live in, but it is the only place we have. I believe also that it has shown us all how our faith – whatever our religion – can inspire us to work together in friendship and peace for the sake of our own and future generations.

15 June 2006

In a lunch given in honour of her 80th birthday at Mansion House, at which she sampled the Great British Menu, the Queen gave thanks for the many birthday wishes she received that year.

My Lord Mayor,

I am most grateful to you for inviting Prince Philip and me to this lunch today to mark both my 80th birthday and the 85th birthday of Prince Philip last weekend.

The Corporation's generous hospitality is well-known, and I have no doubt that this is now even more the case thanks to the 'Great British Menu' which I look forward to sampling shortly.

Creating a good menu is a familiar dilemma for any host, but the solution of competitive cooking is a new concept to me – although I understand there are as yet no penalty shoot-outs.

My Lord Mayor, as one gets older, birthdays seem to come round quicker; they are therefore less obviously excuses for wider celebration than personal moments to count one's blessings.

As Groucho Marx once said 'Anyone can get old – all you have to do is to live long enough'. And there are in my view many other anniversaries this year which are more deserving of celebration.

And as I count my blessings on my birthday I am aware of the value of the advice and encouragement that I am lucky enough to receive from every quarter – from my family, from my friends, from all of you.

My Lord Mayor, I cannot do better than to use this wonderful occasion to express my heartfelt appreciation to the many, many thousands of people from this country and from overseas who have sent me letters, cards and messages of goodwill over the last couple of months.

25 December 2006

The 2006 Christmas message was filmed in Southwark Cathedral in London where the Queen met schoolchildren working on a Nativity collage. The theme of her message that year was understanding between faiths and generations.

The pressures of modern life sometimes seem to be weakening the links which have traditionally kept us together as families and communities. As children grow up and develop their own sense of confidence and independence in the ever-changing technological environment, there is always the danger of a real divide opening up between young and old, based on unfamiliarity, ignorance or misunderstanding.

It is worth bearing in mind that all of our faith communities encourage the bridging of that divide. The wisdom and experience of the great religions point to the need to nurture and guide the young, and to encourage respect for the elderly. It is very easy to concentrate on the differences between the religious faiths and to forget what they have in common – people of different faiths are bound together by the need to help the younger generation to become considerate and active citizens.

And there is another cause for hope that we can do better in the future at bridging the generation gap. As older people remain more active for longer, the opportunities to look for new ways to bring young and old together are multiplying.

As I look back on these past 12 months, marked in particular for me by the very generous response to my 80th birthday, I especially value the opportunities I have had to meet young people. I am impressed by their energy and vitality, and by their ambition to learn and to travel.

It makes me wonder what contribution older people can make to help them realise their ambitions. I am reminded of a lady of about my age who was asked by an earnest, little granddaughter the other day: 'Granny, can you remember the Stone Age?' While that may be going a bit far, the older generation are able to give a sense of context as well as the wisdom of experience which can be invaluable. Such advice and comfort are probably needed more often than younger people admit or older people recognise. I hope that this is something that all of us, young or old, can reflect on at this special time of year.

25 December 2007

The theme of helping the disadvantaged formed the core of the Queen's 2007 Christmas message.

Now today, of course, marks the birth of Jesus Christ. Among other things, it is a reminder that it is the story of a family; but of a family in very distressed circumstances. Mary and Joseph found no room at the inn; they had to make do in a stable, and the new-born Jesus had to be laid in a manger. This was a family which had been shut out.

Perhaps it was because of this early experience that, throughout his ministry, Jesus of Nazareth reached out and made friends with people whom others ignored or despised. It was in this way that he proclaimed his belief that, in the end, we are all brothers and sisters in one human family.

The Christmas story also draws attention to all those people who are on the edge of society – people who feel cut off and disadvantaged; people who, for one reason or another, are not able to enjoy the full benefits of living in a civilised and law-abiding community. For these people the modern world can seem a distant and hostile place.

It is all too easy to 'turn a blind eye', 'to pass by on the other side', and leave it to experts and professionals. All the great religious teachings of the world press home the message that everyone has a responsibility to care for the vulnerable. Fortunately, there are many groups and individuals, often unsung and unrewarded, who are dedicated to ensuring that the 'outsiders' are given a chance to be recognised and respected. However, each one of us can also help by offering a little time, a talent or a possession, and taking a share in the responsibility for the well-being of those who feel excluded.

A familiar introduction to an annual Christmas Carol Service contains the words: 'Because this would most rejoice his heart, let us remember, in his name, the poor and the helpless, the cold, the hungry, and the oppressed; the sick and those who mourn, the lonely and the unloved.'

25 December 2008

In the year that the Prince of Wales celebrated his 60th birthday, the Queen spoke on the theme of being unselfish and using our time and talents to benefit others.

Over the years, those who have seemed to me to be the most happy, contented and fulfilled have always been the people who have lived the most outgoing and unselfish lives; the kind of people who are generous with their talents or their time. There are those who use their prosperity or good fortune for the benefit of others, whether they number among the great philanthropists or are people who, with whatever they have, simply have a desire to help those less fortunate than themselves.

What they offer comes in the form of what can easily be recognised as service to the nation or service to the wider community. As often as not, however, their unselfishness is a simply-taken-for-granted part of the life of their family or neighbourhood.

They tend to have some sense that life itself is full of blessings, and is a precious gift for which we should be thankful. When life seems hard, the courageous do not lie down and accept defeat; instead, they are all the more determined to struggle for a better future.

I think we have a huge amount to learn from individuals such as these. And what I believe many of us share with them is a source of strength and peace of mind in our families and friends. Indeed, Prince Philip and I can reflect on the blessing, comfort and support we have gained from our own family in this special year for our son, The Prince of Wales.

Sixty years ago, he was baptised here in the Music Room at Buckingham Palace. As parents and grandparents, we feel great pride in seeing our family make their own unique contributions to society. Through his charities, The Prince of Wales has worked to support young people and other causes for the benefit of the wider community, and now his sons are following in his footsteps.

I hope that, like me, you will be comforted by the example of Jesus of Nazareth who, often in circumstances of great adversity, managed to live an outgoing, unselfish and sacrificial life.

25 December 2009

The year 2009 marked the 60th anniversary of the creation of the Commonwealth, and the Queen spoke in her Christmas message that year about the organisation and the opportunities it creates for people to work together.

It is sixty years since the Commonwealth was created and today, with more than a billion of its members under the age of 25, the organisation remains a strong and practical force for good. Recently I attended the Commonwealth Heads of Government Meeting in Trinidad and Tobago and heard how important the Commonwealth is to young people.

New communication technologies allow them to reach out to the wider world and share their experiences and viewpoints. For many, the practical assistance and networks of the Commonwealth can give skills, lend advice and encourage enterprise.

It is inspiring to learn of some of the work being done by these young people, who bring creativity and innovation to the challenges they face.

It is important to keep discussing issues that concern us all – there can be no more valuable role for our family of nations.

I have been closely associated with the Commonwealth through most of its existence. The personal and living bond I have enjoyed with leaders, and with people the world over, has always been more important in promoting our unity than symbolism alone. The Commonwealth is not an organisation with a mission. It is rather an opportunity for its people to work together to achieve practical solutions to problems.

In many aspects of our lives, whether in sport, the environment, business or culture, the Commonwealth connection remains vivid and enriching. It is, in lots of ways, the face of the future. And with continuing support and dedication, I am confident that this diverse Commonwealth of nations can strengthen the common bond that transcends politics, religion, race and economic circumstances.

No one has made a greater contribution to the Commonwealth over the decades than the Queen who has been unwavering in her devotion to this Commonwealth family of nations.

CLAIRE WHITAKER OBE,
CHAIR OF THE ROYAL COMMONWEALTH SOCIETY

The End of an Era

2010–2022

After 60 years on the throne and well past retirement age, the Queen showed no signs of slowing down. The final 12 years of Queen Elizabeth's reign saw her take the spotlight to speak on a number of memorable historic occasions. She addressed the United Nations General Assembly in 2010, spoke to the people of Ireland on her first state visit there in 2011, and in 2012 welcomed heads of state from around the world at the beginning of the London Olympic games. As the 2020s dawned she offered the nation words of comfort during the Covid-19 pandemic and celebrated the momentous occasions of the 75-year anniversary of VE Day and her Platinum Jubilee. Her Christmas messages during this time featured topics including the importance of sport in building communities and a touching reflection on bereavement following her husband Prince Philip's death.

6 July 2010

In her first visit since 1957, the Queen addressed the United Nations General Assembly. She celebrated the organisation's achievements and spoke of the work still to be done.

The achievements of the United Nations are remarkable. When I was first here, there were just three United Nations operations overseas. Now over 120,000 men and women are deployed in 26 missions across the world. You have helped to reduce conflict, you have offered humanitarian assistance to millions of people affected by natural disasters and other emergencies, and you have been deeply committed to tackling the effects of poverty in many parts of the world.

But so much remains to be done. Former Secretary-General Dag Hammarskjold once said that 'constant attention by a good nurse may be just as important as a major operation by a surgeon'. Good nurses get better with practice; sadly the supply of patients never ceases.

Since I addressed you last, the Commonwealth, too, has grown vigorously to become a group of nations representing nearly two billion people. It gives its wholehearted support to the significant contributions to the peace and stability of the world made by the United Nations and its agencies. Last November, when I opened the Commonwealth Heads of Government Meeting in Trinidad and Tobago, I told the delegates that the Commonwealth had the opportunity to lead. Today I offer you the same message.

For over six decades the United Nations has helped to shape the international response to global dangers. The challenge now is to continue to show this clear and convening leadership while not losing sight of your ongoing work to secure the security, prosperity and dignity of our fellow human beings.

When people in 53 years from now look back on us, they will doubtless view many of our practices as old-fashioned. But it is my hope that, when judged by future generations, our sincerity, our willingness to take a lead, and our determination to do the right thing will stand the test of time.

In my lifetime, the United Nations has moved from being a high-minded aspiration to being a real force for common good. That of itself has been a signal achievement. But we are not gathered here to reminisce. In tomorrow's world, we must all work together as hard as ever if we are truly to be United Nations.

25 December 2010

In a year which saw athletes compete in the Winter Paralympics and Commonwealth Games, the Queen spoke in her Christmas message about the importance of sport in building communities.

It is as important as ever to build communities and create harmony, and one of the most powerful ways of doing this is through sport and games. During this past year of abundant sporting events, I have seen for myself just how important sport is in bringing people together from all backgrounds, from all walks of life and from all age groups.

In the parks of towns and cities, and on village greens up and down the country, countless thousands of people every week give up their time to participate in sport and exercise of all sorts, or simply encourage others to do so. These kinds of activity are common throughout the world and play a part in providing a different perspective on life.

Apart from developing physical fitness, sport and games can also teach vital social skills. None can be enjoyed without abiding by the rules, and no team can hope to succeed without co-operation between the players. This sort of positive team spirit can benefit communities, companies and enterprises of all kinds.

As the success of recent Paralympics bears witness, a love of sport also has the power to help rehabilitate. One only has to think of the injured men and women of the Armed Forces to see how an interest in games and sport can speed recovery and renew a sense of purpose, enjoyment and comradeship.

Right around the world, people gather to compete under standard rules and, in most cases, in a spirit of friendly rivalry. Competitors know that, to succeed, they must respect their opponents; very often, they like each other too.

18 May 2011

During her first ever visit to Ireland, the Queen gave a speech at Dublin Castle in which she remembered the signing of the Good Friday Agreement and celebrated the two countries' relationship.

Together we have much to celebrate: the ties between our people, the shared values, and the economic, business and cultural links that make us so much more than just neighbours, that make us firm friends and equal partners.

Of course, the relationship has not always been straightforward; nor has the record over the centuries been entirely benign. It is a sad and regrettable reality that through history our islands have experienced more than their fair share of heartache, turbulence and loss.

These events have touched us all, many of us personally, and are a painful legacy. We can never forget those who have died or been injured, and their families. To all those who have suffered as a consequence of our troubled past I extend my sincere thoughts and deep sympathy. With the benefit of historical hindsight we can all see things which we would wish had been done differently or not at all. But it is also true that no one who looked to the future over the past centuries could have imagined the strength of the bonds that are now in place between the governments and the people of our two nations, the spirit of partnership that we now enjoy, and the lasting rapport between us. No one here this evening could doubt that heartfelt desire of our two nations.

What were once only hopes for the future have now come to pass; it is almost exactly 13 years since the overwhelming majority of people in Ireland and Northern Ireland voted in favour of the agreement signed on Good Friday 1998, paving the way for Northern Ireland to become the exciting and inspirational place that it is today. I applaud the work of all those involved in the peace process, and of all those who support and nurture peace.

Many British families have members who live in this country, as many Irish families have close relatives in the United Kingdom. These families share the two islands; they have visited each other and have come home to each other over the years. They are the ordinary people who yearned for the peace and understanding we now have between our two nations and between the communities within those two nations; a living testament to how much in common we have.

These ties of family, friendship and affection are our most precious resource. They are the lifeblood of the partnership across these islands, a golden thread that runs through all our joint successes so far, and all we will go on to achieve. They are a reminder that we have much to do together to build a future for all our grandchildren: the kind of future our grandparents could only dream of.

So we celebrate together the widespread spirit of goodwill and deep mutual understanding that has served to make the relationship more harmonious, close as good neighbours should always be.

WE OFTEN SPEAK OF
THE DEEP AND ENDURING
PARTNERSHIP BETWEEN
OUR TWO COUNTRIES.
IT IS INDEED A SPECIAL
RELATIONSHIP. AND
HER MAJESTY HAS
BEEN A VITAL PART OF
WHAT KEEPS OUR
RELATIONSHIP SO
SPECIAL.

BARACK OBAMA,
PRESIDENT OF THE UNITED STATES OF AMERICA
EXTRACT FROM ITV DOCUMENTARY 'OUR QUEEN AT NINETY', 21 APRIL 2016

24 May 2011

During President Barack Obama's state visit to Britain, the Queen gave a speech in which she celebrated the exchange of people and ideas on various projects, including entertainment and the special relationship between the US and the UK.

Your visit to this country inevitably reminds us of our shared history, our common language, and our strong intellectual and cultural links. It also reminds us that your country twice came to the rescue of the free and democratic world when it was facing military disaster. On each occasion, after the end of those destructive wars, the generosity of the United States made a massive contribution to our economic recovery. Today the United States remains our most important ally and our two nations contribute to the security and prosperity of our peoples, and of the world, through shared national interests.

But our relationship goes far beyond our military and diplomatic ties. In your inaugural address, you spoke to the American people of the values that lay at the heart of your nation's success: 'honesty and hard work, courage and fair play, tolerance and curiosity, loyalty and patriotism'; and of the 'sturdy alliances and enduring convictions' with which your nation had met past challenges and would meet future ones, too. If I may say so, these values underscore much of the life of the United Kingdom also. Together with our alliance, they continue to guide our actions as we confront the challenges of a changing world.

It is unfortunate that there are so many troubles facing the world today, but we are encouraged that in most respects our two countries see these problems in the same light. For this reason we have been able to act together in fields as varied as science, research and higher education to find solutions or to at least make progress towards tackling so many of the social and economic difficulties that confront nations in all parts of the globe.

Entertainment may not be so obviously an example of our close ties, but it forms part of the lives of a great many of our people. Over the years, we have enjoyed some of America's most spectacular musical productions and any number of what we call films – and you might prefer to call movies. In return, British films and theatrical productions have achieved considerable success in your country. This exchange of people and projects has enlarged and invigorated our common language – although I think you will agree we do not always use it in quite the same way!

27 July 2012

At the reception for the heads of government on the opening night of the London Olympic Games, the Queen made a speech praising the athletes and spoke about the journey of the Olympic torch around Britain.

On the occasion of the opening of the London 2012 Olympic Games, Prince Philip and I would like to extend a very warm welcome to you all.

As leaders of the many nations competing in the Games, you have come from around the world to witness this global festival of sport. I hope that you will enjoy your time in the United Kingdom, and I am sure that you will find a warm reception awaiting you, your athletes and the visiting spectators.

This will be the third London Olympiad: my great-grandfather opened the 1908 Games at White City; my father opened the 1948 Games at Wembley Stadium; and later this evening I will take pleasure in declaring open the 2012 London Olympic Games at Stratford, in the east of London.

Over recent months, many in these islands have watched with growing excitement the journey of the Olympic Torch around the United Kingdom. As the Torch has passed through villages and towns it has drawn people together as families and communities. To me, this spirit of togetherness is a most important part of the Olympic ideal; and the British people can be proud of the part they have played in keeping the spirit alive. Many sports played in these Games have their historic roots in this country; and as a nation we have an abiding passion for sport, as well as a tradition of fair play and a good-natured sense of fun.

In all our national Olympics teams there is so much of which we can be proud: groups of young men and women dedicated to excellence and achievement across numerous sporting disciplines. And these teams are ably supported by thousands of organisers, volunteers and supporters who will be following the action not just at the Olympic venues here in the United Kingdom but throughout the world.

For all these reasons, I wish you and your countries a successful, enjoyable and memorable Games.

I HOPE THAT YOU
WILL ENJOY YOUR
TIME IN THE UNITED
KINGDOM, AND I
AM SURE THAT YOU
WILL FIND A WARM
RECEPTION AWAITING
YOU, YOUR ATHLETES
AND THE VISITING
SPECTATORS.

QUEEN ELIZABETH II

25 December 2013

The theme for this year's Christmas message was reflection. Some of the events the Queen herself reflected on were her Diamond Jubilee, the christening of Prince George and the upcoming Commonwealth Games.

I once knew someone who spent a year in a plaster cast recovering from an operation on his back. He read a lot, and thought a lot, and felt miserable.

Later, he realised this time of forced retreat from the world had helped him to understand the world more clearly.

We all need to get the balance right between action and reflection. With so many distractions, it is easy to forget to pause and take stock. Be it through contemplation, prayer, or even keeping a diary, many have found the practice of quiet personal reflection surprisingly rewarding, even discovering greater spiritual depth to their lives.

Reflection can take many forms. When families and friends come together at Christmas, it's often a time for happy memories and reminiscing. Our thoughts are with those we have loved who are no longer with us. We also remember those who through doing their duty cannot be at home for Christmas, such as workers in essential or emergency services.

I myself had cause to reflect this year, at Westminster Abbey, on my own pledge of service made in that great church on Coronation Day sixty years earlier.

The anniversary reminded me of the remarkable changes that have occurred since the Coronation, many of them for the better; and of the things that have remained constant, such as the importance of family, friendship and good neighbourliness.

But reflection is not just about looking back. I and many others are looking forward to the Commonwealth Games in Glasgow next year.

Here at home my own family is a little larger this Christmas.

As so many of you will know, the arrival of a baby gives everyone the chance to contemplate the future with renewed happiness and hope.

In the year ahead, I hope you will have time to pause for moments of quiet reflection. As the man in the plaster cast discovered, the results can sometimes be surprising.

25 December 2014

*In a Christmas message centred around the idea of reconciliation, the
Queen referenced the First World War Christmas truce 100 years ago, the
Commonwealth Games and the Scottish referendum.*

In the ruins of the old Coventry Cathedral is a sculpture of a man and a
woman reaching out to embrace each other. The sculptor was inspired by
the story of a woman who crossed Europe on foot after the war to find her
husband. Casts of the same sculpture can be found in Belfast and Berlin,
and it is simply called 'Reconciliation'.

Reconciliation is the peaceful end to conflict, and we were reminded of
this in August when countries on both sides of the First World War came
together to remember in peace.

In 1914, many people thought the war would be over by Christmas, but sadly
by then the trenches were dug and the future shape of the war in Europe
was set. But, as we know, something remarkable did happen that Christmas,
exactly a hundred years ago today. Without any instruction or command, the
shooting stopped and German and British soldiers met in No Man's Land.
Photographs were taken and gifts exchanged. It was a Christmas truce.

Truces are not a new idea. In the ancient world a truce was declared for
the duration of the Olympic Games and wars and battles were put on
hold. Sport has a wonderful way of bringing together people and nations,
as we saw this year in Glasgow when over seventy countries took part in
the Commonwealth Games. It is no accident that they are known as the
Friendly Games.

Of course, reconciliation takes different forms. In Scotland after the
referendum many felt great disappointment, while others felt great relief;
and bridging these differences will take time.

Sometimes it seems that reconciliation stands little chance in the face of
war and discord. But, as the Christmas truce a century ago reminds us,
peace and goodwill have lasting power in the hearts of men and women.

25 December 2015

In her 2015 Christmas message the Queen spoke about the meaning of the Christmas tree and how it evokes reflection on events past and future, such as her 90th birthday and the 70th anniversary of VJ Day.

The popularity of a tree at Christmas is due in part to my great-great grandparents, Queen Victoria and Prince Albert. After this touching picture was published, many families wanted a Christmas tree of their own, and the custom soon spread.

Gathering round the tree gives us a chance to think about the year ahead – I am looking forward to a busy 2016, though I have been warned I may have Happy Birthday sung to me more than once or twice. It also allows us to reflect on the year that has passed, as we think of those who are far away or no longer with us. Many people say the first Christmas after losing a loved one is particularly hard. But it's also a time to remember all that we have to be thankful for.

One cause for thankfulness this summer was marking seventy years since the end of the Second World War. On VJ Day, we honoured the remaining veterans of that terrible conflict in the Far East, as well as remembering the thousands who never returned.

At the end of that war, the people of Oslo began sending an annual gift of a Christmas tree for Trafalgar Square. It has five hundred lightbulbs and is enjoyed not just by Christians but by people of all faiths, and of none. At the very top sits a bright star, to represent the Star of Bethlehem.

For Joseph and Mary, the circumstances of Jesus's birth – in a stable – were far from ideal, but worse was to come as the family was forced to flee the country.

Despite being displaced and persecuted throughout his short life, Christ's unchanging message was not one of revenge or violence but simply that we should love one another. Although it is not an easy message to follow, we shouldn't be discouraged; rather, it inspires us to try harder: to be thankful for the people who bring love and happiness into our own lives, and to look for ways of spreading that love to others, whenever and wherever we can.

25 December 2016

The theme of this year's Christmas message was inspiration, and the Queen spoke about how meeting unsung heroes had inspired her.

There was a time when British Olympic medal winners became household names because there were so few of them. But the 67 medals at this year's Games in Rio and 147 at the Paralympics meant that the GB medallists' reception at Buckingham Palace was a crowded and happy event. Throughout the Commonwealth there were equally joyful celebrations. Grenada, the Bahamas, Jamaica and New Zealand won more medals per head of population than any other countries.

Many of this year's winners spoke of being inspired by athletes of previous generations. Inspiration fed their aspiration; and having discovered abilities they scarcely knew they had, these athletes are now inspiring others.

A few months ago, I saw inspiration of a different kind when I opened the new Cambridge base of the East Anglian Air Ambulance, where Prince William works as a helicopter pilot. It was not hard to be moved by the dedication of the highly skilled doctors, paramedics and crew, who are called out on average five times a day.

But to be inspirational you don't have to save lives or win medals. I often draw strength from meeting ordinary people doing extraordinary things: volunteers, carers, community organisers and good neighbours; unsung heroes whose quiet dedication makes them special.

They are an inspiration to those who know them, and their lives frequently embody a truth expressed by Mother Teresa, from this year Saint Teresa of Calcutta. She once said, 'Not all of us can do great things. But we can do small things with great love.'

When people face a challenge they sometimes talk about taking a deep breath to find courage or strength. In fact, the word 'inspire' literally means 'to breathe in'. But even with the inspiration of others, it's understandable that we sometimes think the world's problems are so big that we can do little to help. On our own, we cannot end wars or wipe out injustice, but the cumulative impact of thousands of small acts of goodness can be bigger than we imagine.

25 December 2017

On the 60-year anniversary of her first televised Christmas broadcast, the Queen reflected on the concept of 'home'. That year had seen terror attacks in Manchester and the tragic Grenfell Tower fire.

We think of our homes as places of warmth, familiarity and love; of shared stories and memories, which is perhaps why at this time of year so many return to where they grew up. There is a timeless simplicity to the pull of home.

For many, the idea of 'home' reaches beyond a physical building – to a home town or city. This Christmas, I think of London and Manchester, whose powerful identities shone through over the past 12 months in the face of appalling attacks. In Manchester, those targeted included children who had gone to see their favourite singer. A few days after the bombing, I had the privilege of meeting some of the young survivors and their parents.

I describe that hospital visit as a 'privilege' because the patients I met were an example to us all, showing extraordinary bravery and resilience. Indeed, many of those who survived the attack came together just days later for a benefit concert. It was a powerful reclaiming of the ground, and of the city those young people call home.

We expect our homes to be a place of safety – 'sanctuary' even – which makes it all the more shocking when the comfort they provide is shattered. A few weeks ago, The Prince of Wales visited the Caribbean in the aftermath of hurricanes that destroyed entire communities. And here in London, who can forget the sheer awfulness of the Grenfell Tower fire?

Our thoughts and prayers are with all those who died and those who lost so much; and we are indebted to members of the emergency services who risked their own lives, this past year, saving others. Many of them, of course, will not be at home today because they are working, to protect us.

Reflecting on these events makes me grateful for the blessings of home and family, and in particular for 70 years of marriage.

We think of our homes as places of warmth, familiarity and love; of shared stories and memories, which is perhaps why at this time of year so many return to where they grew up.

QUEEN ELIZABETH II

5 April 2020

At a time when the UK and much of the world was in lockdown due to the Covid-19 pandemic, the Queen broadcast a special message in which she thanked the NHS and shared words of hope and reassurance.

I am speaking to you at what I know is an increasingly challenging time. A time of disruption in the life of our country: a disruption that has brought grief to some, financial difficulties to many, and enormous changes to the daily lives of us all.

I want to thank everyone on the NHS front line, as well as care workers and those carrying out essential roles, who selflessly continue their day-to-day duties outside the home in support of us all. I am sure the nation will join me in assuring you that what you do is appreciated and every hour of your hard work brings us closer to a return to more normal times.

I also want to thank those of you who are staying at home, thereby helping to protect the vulnerable and sparing many families the pain already felt by those who have lost loved ones. Together we are tackling this disease, and I want to reassure you that if we remain united and resolute, then we will overcome it.

I hope in the years to come everyone will be able to take pride in how they responded to this challenge. And those who come after us will say that the Britons of this generation were as strong as any. That the attributes of self-discipline, of quiet, good-humoured resolve and of fellow feeling still characterise this country. The pride in who we are is not a part of our past, it defines our present and our future.

The moments when the United Kingdom has come together to applaud its care and essential workers will be remembered as an expression of our national spirit; and its symbol will be the rainbows drawn by children.

Across the Commonwealth and around the world, we have seen heart-warming stories of people coming together to help others, be it through delivering food parcels and medicines, checking on neighbours, or converting businesses to help the relief effort.

And though self-isolating may at times be hard, many people of all faiths, and of none, are discovering that it presents an opportunity to slow down, pause and reflect, in prayer or meditation.

It reminds me of the very first broadcast I made, in 1940, helped by my sister. We, as children, spoke from here at Windsor to children who had been evacuated from their homes and sent away for their own safety. Today, once again, many will feel a painful sense of separation from their loved ones. But now, as then, we know, deep down, that it is the right thing to do.

While we have faced challenges before, this one is different. This time we join with all nations across the globe in a common endeavour, using the great advances of science and our instinctive compassion to heal. We will succeed – and that success will belong to every one of us.

We should take comfort that while we may have more still to endure, better days will return: we will be with our friends again; we will be with our families again; we will meet again.

But for now, I send my thanks and warmest good wishes to you all.

8 May 2020

On the 75th anniversary of VE Day, the Queen addressed the nation at 9 p.m., the exact time her father, King George VI, gave a radio address on VE Day in 1945.

I speak to you today at the same hour as my father did, exactly 75 years ago. His message then was a salute to the men and women at home and abroad who had sacrificed so much in pursuit of what he rightly called a 'great deliverance'.

The war had been a total war; it had affected everyone, and no one was immune from its impact. Whether it be the men and women called up to serve; families separated from each other; or people asked to take up new roles and skills to support the war effort, all had a part to play. At the start, the outlook seemed bleak, the end distant, the outcome uncertain. But we kept faith that the cause was right – and this belief, as my father noted in his broadcast, carried us through.

Never give up, never despair – that was the message of VE Day. I vividly remember the jubilant scenes my sister and I witnessed with our parents and Winston Churchill from the balcony of Buckingham Palace. The sense of joy in the crowds who gathered outside and across the country was profound, though while we celebrated the victory in Europe, we knew there would be further sacrifice. It was not until August that fighting in the Far East ceased and the war finally ended.

Many people laid down their lives in that terrible conflict. They fought so we could live in peace, at home and abroad. They died so we could live as free people in a world of free nations. They risked all so our families and neighbourhoods could be safe. We should and will remember them.

As I now reflect on my father's words and the joyous celebrations, which some of us experienced first hand, I am thankful for the strength and courage that the United Kingdom, the Commonwealth and all our allies displayed.

The wartime generation knew that the best way to honour those who did not come back from the war, was to ensure that it didn't happen again. The greatest tribute to their sacrifice is that countries who were once sworn enemies are now friends, working side by side for the peace, health and prosperity of us all.

Today it may seem hard that we cannot mark this special anniversary as we would wish. Instead we remember from our homes and our doorsteps. But our streets are not empty; they are filled with the love and the care that we have for each other. And when I look at our country today, and see what we are willing to do to protect and support one another, I say with pride that we are still a nation those brave soldiers, sailors and airmen would recognise and admire.

I send my warmest good wishes to you all.

25 December 2020

Christmas 2020 saw many people separated from their loved ones because of social distancing rules during the Covid-19 pandemic. In her message that year the Queen spoke about the way the pandemic had brought people together, and how the efforts of nurses were bringing hope to all.

Every year we herald the coming of Christmas by turning on the lights. And light does more than create a festive mood – light brings hope.

For Christians, Jesus is 'the light of the world', but we can't celebrate his birth today in quite the usual way. People of all faiths have been unable to gather as they would wish for their festivals, such as Passover, Easter, Eid and Vaisakhi. But we need life to go on. Last month, fireworks lit up the sky around Windsor, as Hindus, Sikhs and Jains celebrated Diwali, the festival of lights, providing joyous moments of hope and unity – despite social distancing.

Remarkably, a year that has necessarily kept people apart has, in many ways, brought us closer. Across the Commonwealth, my family and I have been inspired by stories of people volunteering in their communities, helping those in need.

In the United Kingdom and around the world, people have risen magnificently to the challenges of the year, and I am so proud and moved by this quiet, indomitable spirit. To our young people in particular I say thank you for the part you have played.

This year, we celebrated International Nurses' Day, on the 200th anniversary of the birth of Florence Nightingale. As with other nursing pioneers like Mary Seacole, Florence Nightingale shone a lamp of hope across the world. Today, our front-line services still shine that lamp for us – supported by the amazing achievements of modern science – and we owe them a debt of gratitude. We continue to be inspired by the kindness of strangers and draw comfort that – even on the darkest nights – there is hope in the new dawn.

Of course, for many, this time of year will be tinged with sadness: some mourning the loss of those dear to them, and others missing friends and family members distanced for safety, when all they'd really want for Christmas is a simple hug or a squeeze of the hand. If you are among them, you are not alone, and let me assure you of my thoughts and prayers.

REMARKABLY, A YEAR THAT HAS NECESSARILY KEPT PEOPLE APART HAS, IN MANY WAYS, BROUGHT US CLOSER.

QUEEN ELIZABETH II

1 November 2021

In a recorded video address, the Queen welcomed world leaders for the UN Climate Change Conference in Glasgow. She spoke of the importance of working together to tackle the challenges facing the planet.

Thank you, Prime Minister Holness, for your kind words of introduction.

I am delighted to welcome you all to the 26th United Nations Climate Change Conference; and it is perhaps fitting that you have come together in Glasgow, once a heartland of the Industrial Revolution, but now a place to address climate change.

This is a duty I am especially happy to discharge, as the impact of the environment on human progress was a subject close to the heart of my dear late husband, Prince Philip, The Duke of Edinburgh.

I remember well that in 1969, he told an academic gathering:

'If the world pollution situation is not critical at the moment, it is as certain as anything can be, that the situation will become increasingly intolerable within a very short time ... If we fail to cope with this challenge, all the other problems will pale into insignificance.'

It is a source of great pride to me that the leading role my husband played in encouraging people to protect our fragile planet, lives on through the work of our eldest son Charles and his eldest son William. I could not be more proud of them.

Indeed, I have drawn great comfort and inspiration from the relentless enthusiasm of people of all ages – especially the young – in calling for everyone to play their part.

In the coming days, the world has the chance to join in the shared objective of creating a safer, stabler future for our people and for the planet on which we depend.

None of us underestimates the challenges ahead: but history has shown that when nations come together in common cause, there is always room for hope. Working side by side, we have the ability to solve the most insurmountable problems and to triumph over the greatest of adversities.

For more than seventy years, I have been lucky to meet and to know many of the world's great leaders. And I have perhaps come to understand a little about what made them special.

It has sometimes been observed that what leaders do for their people today is government and politics. But what they do for the people of tomorrow – that is statesmanship.

I, for one, hope that this conference will be one of those rare occasions where everyone will have the chance to rise above the politics of the moment, and achieve true statesmanship.

It is the hope of many that the legacy of this summit – written in history books yet to be printed – will describe you as the leaders who did not pass up the opportunity; and that you answered the call of those future generations. That you left this conference as a community of nations with a determination, a desire and a plan, to address the impact of climate change; and to recognise that the time for words has now moved to the time for action.

Of course, the benefits of such actions will not be there to enjoy for all of us here today: we none of us will live forever. But we are doing this not for ourselves but for our children and our children's children, and those who will follow in their footsteps.

And so, I wish you every good fortune in this significant endeavour.

AND FOR ME AND MY FAMILY, EVEN WITH ONE FAMILIAR LAUGH MISSING THIS YEAR, THERE WILL BE JOY IN CHRISTMAS, AS WE HAVE THE CHANCE TO REMINISCE, AND SEE ANEW THE WONDER OF THE FESTIVE SEASON THROUGH THE EYES OF OUR YOUNG CHILDREN.

QUEEN ELIZABETH II

25 December 2021

In her 2021 Christmas message, the Queen gave special mention to those who had lost loved ones, including herself, after the loss of her husband. It was her final Christmas broadcast.

Although it's a time of great happiness and good cheer for many, Christmas can be hard for those who have lost loved ones. This year, especially, I understand why.

But for me, in the months since the death of my beloved Philip, I have drawn great comfort from the warmth and affection of the many tributes to his life and work – from around the country, the Commonwealth and the world. His sense of service, intellectual curiosity and capacity to squeeze fun out of any situation were all irrepressible. That mischievous, enquiring twinkle was as bright at the end as when I first set eyes on him.

But life, of course, consists of final partings as well as first meetings; and as much as I and my family miss him, I know he would want us to enjoy Christmas.

We felt his presence as we, like millions around the world, readied ourselves for Christmas. While Covid again means we can't celebrate quite as we may have wished, we can still enjoy the many happy traditions.

I am sure someone somewhere today will remark that Christmas is a time for children. It's an engaging truth, but only half the story. Perhaps it's truer to say that Christmas can speak to the child within us all. Adults, when weighed down with worries, sometimes fail to see the joy in simple things, where children do not.

And for me and my family, even with one familiar laugh missing this year, there will be joy in Christmas, as we have the chance to reminisce, and see anew the wonder of the festive season through the eyes of our young children, of whom we were delighted to welcome four more this year.

They teach us all a lesson – just as the Christmas story does – that in the birth of a child, there is a new dawn with endless potential.

5 June 2022

In 2022, Britain marked the Platinum Jubilee in style, with events held up and down the country. At the end of the weekend's celebrations, the Queen delivered a thank you message.

When it comes to how to mark seventy years as your Queen, there is no guidebook to follow. It really is a first. But I have been humbled and deeply touched that so many people have taken to the streets to celebrate my Platinum Jubilee.

While I may not have attended every event in person, my heart has been with you all; and I remain committed to serving you to the best of my ability, supported by my family.

I have been inspired by the kindness, joy and kinship that has been so evident in recent days, and I hope this renewed sense of togetherness will be felt for many years to come.

I thank you most sincerely for your good wishes and for the part you have all played in these happy celebrations.

THE QUEEN WAS INCOMPARABLY PROFESSIONAL. SHE HAD A VERY, VERY CLEAR IDEA OF WHAT THE SOVEREIGN OF THIS COUNTRY SHOULD DO. SHE BECAME MORE AND MORE SKILLED AT MAINTAINING A POSITION, MAINTAINING A WAY OF BEHAVING AND SPEAKING, AND OF MASTERING A BRIEF AND DOING A JOB WITH CONVICTION.

DAVID ATTENBOROUGH,
WHO WORKED WITH THE QUEEN ON HER CHRISTMAS BROADCASTS,
AFTER HER DEATH, SEPTEMBER 2022

ꟷNDEX OF SPEECHES

INDEX